SIGNALS

A RAILWAY MISCELLANY

HERTFORDSHIRE, BUCKINGHAMSHIRE AND BEDFORDSHIRE

MURRAY ECKETT

First published September 2008 by
Book Castle Publishing
2a Sycamore Business Park
Copt Hewick
North Yorkshire HG4 5DF

ISBN 978 1 903747 90 2

Designed and typeset by Tracey Moren, Moren Associates Limited
www.morenassociates.co.uk

Printed in Malta by Poultons Print.

Front cover illustration: Heath Park Halt Station, Hemel Hempstead. Teatime departure to Harpenden headed by LMS Class 3F 0-6-0 3245 on the "Nickey" line. (From a painting by Alan Ward; copyright and publisher; Sidelines Gallery.)

INTRODUCTION

How did this book come about? It was during the summer of 1970 that my lifelong interest in trains and railways began, during a family holiday to Barmouth, in North Wales. The guest house at which we stayed backed on to the then British Rail line between Dovey Junction and Pwllheli, and located nearby were two of the famous "Great Little Trains of Wales", the lines in question being the Talyllyn and Fairbourne Railways, both of which were visited during the course of that long ago holiday. The events of this holiday sparked off my fascination with all things railway, beginning with the collection of various books and magazines. The following Christmas was marked by my being given my first train set, the locomotive being none other than "Flying Scotsman", which I still possess to this day.

During the mid 1980s, having attended a number of meetings of the St Albans Locomotive Club of Great Britain (LCGB) at Chiswell Green, near to the cathedral city, I was offered the chance to join the Branch Committee, the position that I was asked to fill being that of publicity officer. One of the ways that I decided to try and make the Branch better known to a wider audience was to write articles on local railways, which featured a "plug" for the Branch. The first of these articles was published in 1988, and, since then, I have been lucky enough to have seen a number of my jottings in print, with a great amount of help and encouragement from Beaumonde Publications, the owners of "Hertfordshire Countryside" and the former "Buckinghamshire Countryside" county magazines. From these articles came the idea to revise and collect these essays together, plus a series of new chapters, the result being the publication of this book. I have enjoyed researching, writing and putting together this book; I hope that you get as much pleasure from reading it.

ACKNOWLEDGEMENTS

During the writing of this book, I have been very fortunate in obtaining help from many different sources. This help consisted mainly of cross-checking a number of the chapters within these covers. Allan Baker (Marketing Manager for the Buckinghamshire Railway Centre) looked at the articles about the BRC itself, Verney Junction, and the Brill Branch, whilst Roger Fagg (Chairman of the Chinnor & Princes Risborough Railway) did the same for the CPRR essay. Mervyn Leah (Chairman, Leighton Buzzard Narrow Gauge Railway) cast his eye over the chapter about the LBNGR and its predecessors, whilst Ron Stanbridge, the manager of the Fancott Miniature Railway, was most helpful with advice and information about this developing attraction. I was also grateful for help from three of my Locomotive Club of Great Britain (LCGB) colleagues, Jack Turner (Club Chairman), Bryan Cross (Bedford Branch Chairman), and Peter Lawrence (St Albans Branch Treasurer and Historian), for looking at my articles about these three sections of the Club. John Sugars (Chairman of the Rushden Historic Transport Society) cross checked the chapter about the Wellingborough to Higham Ferrers branch line. Roger Green (LCGB St Albans Fixtures Co-ordinator) was kind enough to lend me a series of books for research purposes. I would also like to acknowledge the help given by Mr Derrick Farman, the owner of the former station house at Stanbridgeford station, for showing me over his premises. As regards the historical photographs used, I would like to thank all those who allowed me permission to use their pictures within the covers of this book, in particular Alan Ward, who painted the wonderful illustration that I used for the front cover. Last, but by no means least, I would like to thank Mrs Barbara Shortall (St Albans LCGB Minutes Secretary) for typing up the original manuscript for the majority of these articles.

ABOUT THE AUTHOR

Murray Eckett was born in Hemel Hempstead in 1964, and still lives in the town today. He has been interested in trains and railways from an early age. Railways play a large part in Murray's working life, in his capacity as a train spares buyer for Metronet Rail. Since 1986, he has been carrying out voluntary work on behalf of the Locomotive Club of Great Britain (LCGB) carrying out two publicity officer roles, one each for the St Albans LCGB and the national organisation of the same name. In the course of his essay writing on behalf of the St Albans LCGB, the idea for this book was born, this being his first such work. Apart from railways, Murray is also interested in aviation, in particular historical aircraft, and also enjoys watching both football and cricket.

CONTENTS

BUCKINGHAMSHIRE 115

BEDFORDSHIRE

BIBLIOGRAPHY

HERTFORDSHIRE

Forgotten Railways; Chilterns & Cotswolds (Authors; R.Davies and M.D.Grant). Publisher; David & Charles.

Chiltern Railways Remembered (Author; Leslie Oppitz). Publisher; Countryside Books.

Railways Through The Chilterns (Author; C.R.L.Coles). Publisher; Ian Allan.

British Railways Pre-Grouping Atlas. Publisher; Ian Allan.

The Harpenden to Hemel Hempstead Railway (Authors; Sue and Geoff Woodward). Publisher; Oakwood Press.

The Hatfield and St Albans Branch (Authors; Roger D.Taylor and Brian Anderson). Publisher; Oakwood Press.

The Hatfield, Luton, and Dunstable Railway (Authors; Sue and Geoff Woodward). Publisher; Oakwood Press.

Welwyn's Railways (Authors; Tom Gladwin, Peter Neville and Douglas White). Publisher; Castlemead.

The Life and Times of the Great Eastern Railway (Authors; Harry Parr and Adrian Gray). Publisher; Castlemead.

1897 Ordnance Survey Map of Hemel Hempstead.

1897 Ordnance Survey Map of Boxmoor.

BUCKINGHAMSHIRE

Forgotten Railways;Chilterns & Cotswolds (Authors; R.Davies and M.D.Grant). Publisher; David & Charles.

Chiltern Railways Remembered (Author; Leslie Oppitz). Publisher; Countryside Books.

British Railways Pre-Grouping Atlas. Publisher; Ian Allan.

The Story of Chinnor Station (Author; Marguerita Best). Publishers; Chinnor & Princes Risborough Railway (CPPR).

CPPR; A Visitor's Guide.

Buckinghamshire Railway Centre; A Visitor's Guide.

Watching The Trains At Brill (Author; Robert Avery). Publisher;

Robert Avery.

The Last Days of Steam in Buckinghamshire (Author; John Healy). Publisher; Alan Sutton.

BEDFORDSHIRE

Forgotten Railways; Chilterns & Cotswolds (Authors; R.Davies and M.D.Grant). Publisher; David & Charles.

Chiltern Railways Remembered (Author; Leslie Oppitz). Publisher; Countryside Books.

British Railways Pre-Grouping Atlas. Publisher; Ian Allan.

Railways in Bedfordshire on old picture postcards (Author; Sandy Chrystal). Publisher; Reflections of a Bygone Age.

Personal Reflections of the Bedford-Hitchin Railway (Author; Peter Waylett). Publisher; Peter Waylett.

LCGB Bedford Branch 1958-1998. Publisher; LCGB Bedford Branch.

Leighton Buzzard Narrow Gauge Railway; A Visitor's Guide.

A History of the Railways of Northamptonshire (Author; Peter Butler). Publisher; The Nostalgia Collection.

Forgotten Railways; East Anglia (Author; R.S. Joby). Publisher; David & Charles.

British Railways Past and Present, Volume 24 (Author; Paul Shannon). Publisher; Past & Present Collection.

The Leighton Buzzard Narrow Gauge Railway (Author; Sidney Leleux). Publisher; Oakwood Press.

The Whipsnade and Umfolozi Railway (Author; C.S.Thomas). Publisher; Oakwood Press

The Railway Age in Bedfordshire (Author; Fred Cockman). Publisher; The Book Castle.

Ordnance Survey Map 152; Northampton and Milton Keynes.

Ordnance Survey Map 153; Bedford and Huntingdon.

Ordnance Survey Map 165; Leighton Buzzard.

Ordnance Survey Map 166; Luton.

HERTFORDSHIRE

Park Street Station. Judging by the signs and the uniforms, this picture would have been taken during the Edwardian period (1901-14).
(Courtesy; RAS Marketing/Photomatic).

NATIONAL RAILWAY SYSTEM

*A special tour of Underground lines, formed of a Cravens built tube train,
is seen at Watford (Met) in April 2000. (MJE).*

THE ABBEY FLYER

THE WATFORD JUNCTION TO ST ALBANS ABBEY BRANCH LINE

The Watford Junction to St Albans Abbey branch line, a service currently provided by London Midland Train Operating Company (TOC), has had an unremarkable existence over the years since it was first opened for passenger traffic in May 1858. However, and unsurprisingly, the line has been threatened with closure on occasions, and cutbacks have had to be made in order to reduce running costs. At the present moment in time, the line is on something of an upward spiral, one of the main reasons for this happy state of affairs being the complete electrification of the six-and-a-half mile route during 1987/8.

The changes that have taken place at Watford Junction since the 1960s mean that services to St Albans Abbey now depart from platform eleven. This rather exposed part of the Junction is reached via the station subway, which has been refurbished since the beginning of the previous TOC franchise, up a set of steps, and along a narrow footpath to the platform itself. Potential passengers have a waiting room to use. A resurfaced platform, together with new protective fencing, gives customers the impression of a railway line that wants to be in the 21st century, although it is a world away from the sleek "Pendelino" trains that race through the main line platforms. Looking over the fence, the scene is dominated by a multi storey car park, part of the facilities that have been constructed on the site of the former engine sheds. Amongst the many steam locomotives that were prepared there, were the engines that plied back and forth to the Abbey over many years, these being of Webb, Ivatt and Fowler design, amongst others.

*A northbound rugby excursion is seen at Watford Junction during the 1950s.
In the right background can be seen a London Transport Bakerloo line
service, formed of 1938 built tube rolling stock.
(Courtesy; R.S.Carpenter Collection).*

*Stanier designed "Jubilee" locomotive 45559 " British Columbia" passes
Watford Junction on a Euston-Manchester passenger train circa 1955-6.
(Courtesy; R.S.Carpenter Collection).*

The beginning (or end?) of the Abbey Flyer route, Watford Junction's platform eleven, viewed in 1992. (MJE).

A 1992 view along the overgrown exit footpath from Watford Junction's platform eleven to the station subway. The situation has improved since then, with both footpath and subway having been refurbished. (MJE).

The landscape at this point is dominated by the industrial area of north Watford. Leaving the Junction, the line cuts something of a swathe through groups of warehouses of various types. The train has a journey of less than one mile before arriving at the single platform at Watford North. As with all the stations along the line, the facilities are painted in the house colours of the previous franchise holder Silverlink, these being lime green and purple. A brick shelter exists for the comfort of potential users. Leaving Watford North, it would seem that the level crossing just beyond the station marks a division between industrial north Watford and the houses and flats that make up Garston. A reminder of some of the freight traffic that was carried along the branch in the prosperous past comes at this point, as traces can be seen of the trackwork that once led to the old Watford coal depot, which was closed in the 1970s. An overgrown siding still extends almost as far as Garston station itself. The old sits at this point alongside the new, as the nearby hypermarket extends almost to the side of the line boundary.

BR Standard 2-6-4 tank locomotive 80036 is seen at the Watford Junction locomotive sheds, during the late 1950s. This shed has since been closed, demolished, and the site is now the station car park.
(Courtesy; R.S.Carpenter Collection).

An experimental diesel multiple unit (DMU) that was built by the British United Traction Company is seen at Watford Junction during the 1950s. This unit was very rough riding, and was withdrawn from service after a short space of time. (Courtesy; TLOSA).

Garston station is of a similar layout to that of Watford North, comprising a single platform and shelter. It was opened as recently as 1966, in order to serve the expanding housing estate there, and was almost unique insomuch as it was constructed at a time when much of the national railway system was being run down and closed. It was brought into service only three years after the infamous "Beeching Report" had listed the "Flyer" for closure.

Beyond Garston, the line quickly leaves the outskirts of Watford, and is soon surrounded by the lush Hertfordshire countryside. This section of line as far as Bricket Wood is the longest without a station stop, and is perhaps the most scenic, with many trees overhanging the line. The route passes under the M1 motorway at this point, whilst running parallel with Park Street Lane for the majority of the remaining journey to the Abbey. Nearing Bricket Wood, more houses come into view, until the train slows for the stop there. The station building at Bricket Wood is the most impressive on the line. In times past, a passing loop was installed at this point, and a second platform was in situ on the opposite side of the track. However, the economies made in the 1960s changed the station to its present layout. The building itself has suffered from the effects of vandalism and the graffiti artists over the years. However, at the time of writing, the building was graffiti free and in a reasonable state of repair. The station yard has found a new function, playing host to a builder's merchants.

A busy scene at Bricket Wood, on the Watford Jct-St Albans Abbey line 30/4/1955. On the left is an RCTS special, the nearest coach being a Gresley design, whilst on the right is the experimental British United Traction DMU, working the normal service train. (Courtesy; Mr T.J.Edgington).

Leaving Bricket Wood, the train crosses the M25 motorway, before arriving at the newest station on the line, How Wood. This station was opened in 1988, at the time of the line's electrification, and is laid out in a similar way to Garston and Watford North, with a single platform containing a small waiting room for use by passengers. Unfortunately, the station has suffered on occasions from the effects of vandalism. However, at the time of writing, it seemed in a healthy state of repair.

Bricket Wood station circa 1990, looking towards St Albans, and showing to good advantage the substantial station building. (MJE).

Ex LNWR Webb 2-4-2T 6725 propelling the 15.55 Watford-St Albans local train at Bricket Wood 5/9/1947. (Courtesy; LCGB Ken Nunn Collection).

11

How Wood station in 1990 looking towards Watford
from the approach road foot crossing. (MJE).

A train approaching St Albans hauled by an LNWR tank engine.
(Courtesy; R.S.Carpenter Photographs).

Leaving How Wood, the train quickly arrives at Park Street, after crossing both Park Street Lane and the A5 road. Just before Park Street Lane, a connecting line was built during the 1860s in order to carry goods trains that were being used in the construction of the Midland Railway's line into London St Pancras, this being completed in 1868. The connecting line itself was abandoned shortly afterwards, although the embankment used can still be seen in the park that extends from the right hand side of the Abbey line down to the A5 road.

Park Street is laid out in much the same way as most of the other stations on the line. The platform and shelter are in good condition, whilst some of the former goods yard has been resurfaced, and the rest given over to new housing. As with St Albans Abbey station, Park Street is a mere shadow of its former self, the impressive buildings that were in situ having been demolished in order to cut back on running costs.

A 1990 view of Park Street station, looking towards St Albans Abbey. The predominance of red seats, shelters, etc, in this series of pictures shows that the line was then part of British Rail's Network South East sector.
(MJE).

13

Park Street Station again, this time in the 1950s BR era. The "totem" station signs give the date away. (Courtesy; RAS Marketing/Photomatic).

Leaving Park Street, the train dives into a cutting, and gradually curves around in a northerly direction. The scene from the train at this point of the journey is one of contrast, with a rural part of the countryside being noted to the right hand side, whilst the left hand side is gradually filled with more and more houses as the terminus is approached. Coming into St Albans Abbey, it is easy to note the right hand bay platform that was the beginning of the long closed line to Hatfield, now converted into a public footpath. Dominating the scene at this point of the journey is a single gas-holder, the last remaining part of the former gas works. Much of the site of the works, and that of of the extensive railway sidings, has been swallowed up by various superstores. A further section of land was sold by the railway to a consortium for building a series of office blocks alongside the line, and these back onto the bottom of Holywell Hill.

As mentioned before, the Abbey station has been reduced to a very basic single platform station to reduce running costs. In recent times however, much has been done to improve the station's appearance. A car park has been provided next to the platform, along with an improved waiting shelter and a covered bicycle rack. As at all the stations, improved lighting is very much in evidence. The overall impression is of a station that is "welcoming", thereby encouraging people to travel.

What of the future? It is worth mentioning at this point the sterling work done by two organisations, the line's passenger user group, "ABFLY", and the Abbey Line Community Rail Partnership. Both these groups have done much to raise the line's profile, both in the local community and further afield. It was interesting to note that, at each station, an information board had been provided, giving details of public transport connections. Such initiatives can only encourage more people to forsake their cars for the "Flyer". Plans are afoot to re-introduce the Bricket Wood loop (thus doubling the frequency of the train service), and there has been talk of having through trains to London Euston. However,

A 1992 view of St Albans Abbey, looking towards Watford Junction. The overgrown bay platform to the left was the start of the Great Northern Railway's branch line to Hatfield, the bulk of which is now a public footpath. (MJE).

time will tell whether these improvements will happen. For the moment, the future of the line looks assured.

Website Addresses:

Abbey Line Community Rail Partnership - www.abbeyline.org.uk

Abbey Flyer Users Group (ABFLY) - www.abfly.org.uk

St Albans Abbey in the summer of 1955. An LMS Fowler designed 2-6-2T 40048 arrives under the long since demolished station canopy. On the right can be seen some wagons, these being used to transport coal to and from the adjacent gasworks. (Courtesy; A.W.V.Mace/Milepost 92 1/2 collection).

NORTHERN EXTENSIONS

CHALFONT & LATIMER TO CHESHAM
MOOR PARK TO AMERSHAM
WATFORD (MET) TO MOOR PARK

The Metropolitan Line of today's complex London Underground (LUL) railway network is a vital transport artery, one of thirteen such lines that combine to make up the system that helps to keep London on the move. Yet, until 1936, this line was a fully independent railway company, providing both passenger and goods services to large parts of Hertfordshire, Buckinghamshire and Middlesex.

The original section of the Metropolitan Railway's (MR) main claim to fame was that it was the first underground railway to be opened in the world. In January 1863, the section of line between Paddington (Bishops Road) and Farringdon Street was brought into use. Despite the bad atmospheric conditions that were found in the tunnels (due to the fact that the service was entirely worked by steam locomotives) , the new line was a great success. The underground network was quickly expanded, and the whole of what is now known as the Circle Line was completed as early as October 1884.

It was not long before the MR began to look at extending their lincs into new territory north of London. They were helped in their plans by the formation of an independent railway company known as the Metropolitan and St Johns Wood Railway (M & SJWR). This new organisation opened its initial section of track between Baker Street and Swiss Cottage in April 1868. Its rolling stock was supplied by the MR, who also owned a large number of shares in the smaller railway company. As with the MR, the smaller company had a successful early life, and by 1879 it had reached West Hampstead by way of Finchley

Road. A further extension to Harrow-on-the-Hill was completed in August 1880. However, the M & SJWR remained a tempting takeover target for the MR, and in 1883 its short independent life came to an end when it became part of the larger railway.

It was in the last twenty years of the nineteenth century that the MR started to expand in a big way, initially crossing into the counties of Hertfordshire and Buckinghamshire. A most go-ahead individual, Mr (later Sir) Edward Watkin, had become MR chairman and his long term goal was to utilise his new line as part of a grand scheme to build a railway route between Manchester and Paris, via a Channel Tunnel link. As well as the MR, Mr Watkin had major interests in what became the Great Central Railway, which joined Manchester with London Marylebone in 1897, and the South East and Chatham Railway, which linked London with Dover.

The MR's expansion continued, and it reached the town of Chesham in July 1889. At the time this was the terminus of the MR's main line from London. It did not become the branch line that it is today until 1892, when the northbound extension to Aylesbury was completed. In the original MR plans, Chesham station was due to be sited some distance from the town centre, due to problems incurred in obtaining the necessary land. However, in contrast to what generally happened with other railway building schemes, this plan was objected to by prominent members of the local community. They felt so strongly that the new station should be located near to the town centre that they decided to pool their monetary resources and buy the piece of land upon which the present day station now stands. Since the time of those pioneering days, the four mile line from Chesham to Chalfont has had an unremarkable existence, typical of many similar lines all over Britain. To begin with, steam traction was used until 1960, apart from a short visit by an experimental diesel multiple unit (DMU) during 1952. This was not a success, due to excessive vibration by the DMU when running in service. However, in September 1960, electric traction came to the line as part of the modernisation of the by now Metropolitan Line (the original Metropolitan Railway Company having become part of London

Transport in 1936). Although it meant the end of everyday steam working, the electrification secured the long term future of the line. However, in an enlightened piece of corporate policy, steam traction returned to the line in 1989 to mark its centenary, hauling a series of special trains.

A May 1989 picture taken at Chesham. The occasion was the 100th anniversary of the opening of the original Metropolitan Railway (MR) extension to this location. The electric locomotive depicted is named "Sarah Siddons". It was one of twenty similar engines built for the MR from 1922 onwards, and is one of only two still surviving today, "John Hampden" being the other, now to be found in the LT Museum at Covent Garden. (MJE).

The early 1890s saw the northbound extension of the MR being continued. The "main line" headed north from the station of Chalfont Road (now renamed Chalfont and Latimer) to Aylesbury via Amersham. The new section of line was opened to the public in September 1892. Amersham station itself was renamed Amersham and Chesham Bois between 1922 and 1934. In September 1961, as part of the Metropolitan modernisation plans, it became the terminus of all LT services, whilst

LMSR Fowler designed 2-6-4 tank locomotive 42351 seen at Chesham circa late 1950s. (Courtesy; A.Scarsbrook/Initial Photographics).

the responsibility for trains north of Amersham became that of British Railways. A little known fact is that Amersham is the highest station on the whole of the LUL network, being four hundred and ninety feet above mean sea level.

The third section of line that helps to form this chapter, the branch between Watford (Met) and the main MR line between Rickmansworth and Moor Park was a much later addition to the tube network, not being opened until late in 1925. This was in spite of the fact that the earliest proposal for such a route had been drawn up some thirty years previously in 1895. The 2.5 mile line was a joint project between the MR and the London and North Eastern Railway (LNER). It was worked as a joint concern from the line's opening in November 1925 to the time of the General Strike in 1926, after which the LNER withdrew from the previous arrangements. There were plans to build beyond Watford (Met), through Cassiobury Park, to a new terminus in Watford town centre. The MR had even earmarked a suitable building to serve as the main station entrance; this was to be found at no 44 Watford High Street.

Chorleywood station depicted in January 1998, looking in the direction of Chalfont and Latimer. This station is served by two separate train companies; the electric trains of the Metropolitan line, and the diesels of Chiltern Railways. (MJE).

However, this bold scheme was never followed through, although the building itself survives to this day and is now a public house.

In the course of travelling over these three sections of line today, there is much of interest that can still be found. Passengers arriving at Chalfont and Latimer will find an old fashioned bay platform, which marks the beginning of the branch line to Chesham. The most obvious difference to the casual observer is that, while main line "Met" services are operated by eight car sets made up of the rugged and reliable "A" class electric multiple units, a four car train is sufficient for the Chesham link. Trains are run at thirty minute intervals, and nine minutes are allowed for the four mile run. Leaving Chalfont, the branch parallels the main line to Amersham to begin with before the line curves away to the right. A mixture of houses and industrial units crowd upon the track, before breathtaking countryside is reached; glorious views of the surrounding area can be seen looking away from the right hand side of the Chesham-bound train. It is hard to believe that, within fifty minutes journey time, a similar type of train can be used to pass through the centre of London. The line then passes into a shallow cutting, surrounded by tall trees, before the outskirts of Chesham are reached, a further selection of industrial units and houses marking the town boundary.

Chesham station, as with most of the stations on this part of the "Met", retains a charming olde-world atmosphere, entirely in keeping with its surroundings. MR architecture is still in evidence, as is a well made water tower, a steam age necessity for thirsty engines that had made their way from Chalfont. A signalbox can still be found on the opposite side of the station to the main platform. Although not in use, this is a reminder of times past, as is the existence of the bay platform, now finding new life as the station garden.

Returning to the MR "main line", as mentioned before, Amersham

An exterior view of Chesham, the terminus of the branch line from Chalfont & Latimer. Taken in June 1997. (MJE).

*An interior view, taken at the same time as the previous picture. The
station feels semi-rural, rather than a part of the oldest and most complex
underground railway network in the world. (MJE).*

is the current northern terminus of all LUL services. The Underground
trains share the three platforms with those of Chiltern Railways, whose
modern diesel multiple unit trains provide regular services for stations
to Aylesbury, and, in some cases, as far as Birmingham Moor Street.
Underground services have a frequency of four trains per hour to and
from the capital, except at peak hours when the service becomes more
intensive. The short journey as far as Moor Park passes through a trio
of stations, these being Chalfont, Chorleywood, and Rickmansworth,
before the short run past the triangular junction with the Watford Met
branch, and into Moor Park itself.

Moor Park station presents a much more modern appearance to the
traveller than the other stations mentioned so far in this chapter. It was
modernised in the early 1960s, as part of the LT upgrading programme
that was carried out on the Met at this time. The origins of the station go

An exterior view of Amersham station, taken in June 2004. This is the terminus of the Metropolitan line's service from Aldgate and Baker Street. In the background can be seen one of the line's hard working "A" stock trains. These units, originally built by Cravens in Sheffield, have been in revenue earning service nearly fifty years, having first been introduced into LT service in 1960. (MJE).

back to 1910, when a small halt, Sandy Lodge, was built and opened, mainly for the benefit of people wishing to use the nearby Moor Park golf course. Following the end of the First World War, the Moor Park housing estate began to be constructed, and, with the opening of the Watford branch in 1925, Sandy Lodge became Moor Park. The 1960s rebuilding of the station was in conjunction with the construction of two extra sets of running lines, in order to separate LT trains from those of the British Railways route into Marylebone.

Leaving Moor Park, Watford bound travellers head in a northerly direction, passing the Moor Park industrial estate on the right hand side, and accessing the branch itself via one side of the triangular junction mentioned above. The remains of Watford Tip are passed at

A second exterior view of Amersham, also taken in June 2004, this time looking towards London. (MJE).

this point where, until the early 1970s, LT used former Great Western Railway steam locomotives for shunting duties. Trains pass through a tall cutting, and under a road bridge, before arriving at Croxley station. This establishment is made up of two platforms, plus a solid overbridge, giving passengers access from the booking hall, which is at street level. A large car park gives the impression of a great number of daily users; in fact the station is one of the lesser used on the whole of the tube network. Leaving Croxley, the line passes an increasing number of houses, before arriving at Watford Met. This part of the line is intended to be one side of the "Croxley Link", a plan to join the route with the former Network Rail branch from Croxley Green to Watford Junction. Hopefully, after many false starts, this bold project will become fact before too many more years have passed.

Watford Met itself is made up of a single island platform, and the station building is of the same "Met" type design as that at Croxley. The

An exterior view of the entrance to Croxley underground station
in June 1997. (MJE).

fact that the line runs only as far as the Cassiobury Park estate ensures that it has become something of a quiet backwater, although regular buses and taxis are always on hand to take the would-be traveller into Watford itself, and the service from here to Baker Street has an impressive frequency of ten minutes. The old goods yard has now vanished under a new housing development adjacent to the right hand side of the line. What may have been its busiest day ever occurred in May 1999, when Watford played Bolton in the Football League Championship Play-Off Final at the old Wembley stadium. The author can recall seeing a queue extending a long way back up the road towards the junction with the A412 to Rickmansworth; this queue being the best part of a mile long.

The three sections of line which have been outlined in this chapter are, by themselves, quite unremarkable. However, in the current scheme of things, they all make their own special contribution to the well-being of both the tube network and the local economy. However, it is most interesting to reflect on the fact that if things had been a little different, they could have been part of a "Eurostar" network some one hundred years before the present London-Paris-Brussels service came into being.

HERTFORDSHIRE CITY LINK

HIGH BARNET TO HIGHGATE

To anyone unfamiliar with the layout of the London Underground railway system, it may seem strange that several locations in the county of Hertfordshire are served by this vast transport system. In fact, there are a number of local towns that can be found on the tube network, these including Watford, Cockfosters (which is located near to Potters Bar), and High Barnet, which forms part of the subject of this chapter. The line from High Barnet to Highgate is a part of the Northern Line of London Underground, and, as such, provides a vital link for many thousands of passengers who wish to travel to Central London, either for business or pleasure.

The story of this particular section of line begins as far back as 1867. On the 22nd of August of that year, the railway line between Finsbury Park and Edgware was opened by the fledgling Edgware and Highgate Railway Company. Included within this line was the present day section of track between East Finchley and Mill Hill East. As with many early railway companies, the E & HRC was taken over by a larger concern, this being the then-rapidly expanding Great Northern Railway (GNR), who soon added a second branch line between Finchley Crouch End (now known as Finchley Central) and High Barnet. This new line was opened for traffic in April 1872. These two branch lines would probably have led the same kind of unremarkable existence as many similar railway routes up and down the country, had it not been for the intervention of the London Passenger Transport Board (LPTB) during the 1930s.

The LPTB (or London Transport as it soon became widely known) was formed in July 1933, and the new company's board of directors was quick to note opportunities for expansion at several points on the tube network. A programme was drawn up to implement these schemes, and this was known as the 1935-1940 "New Works Programme". Under this scheme, the system's Northern Line would benefit by an extension of the tube network from the boundary at the present day Archway station to a new interchange at East Finchley, with the London and North Eastern Railway (LNER) branch lines to Finsbury Park and Alexandra Palace. The tube electrification programme would then be extended as far as High Barnet. At the same time, the line between Finchley Central and Edgware would also be electrified, and the track doubled. The existing LNER station at Edgware would be closed, and trains would be concentrated on the newer Edgware tube station, which had opened for traffic in 1924. Due to the beginning of the Second World War in 1939, only part of these grand plans was actually carried out. The section of line between Archway and East Finchley was electrified in July 1939, with the High Barnet section being completed in April 1940. The line to Edgware from Finchley Central was partially electrified (this being finished in 1941) only as far as Mill Hill East, for the benefit of the military barracks located there. Work on the remainder of the line from Mill Hill to Edgware ceased at this time. In due course the branch was closed, and replaced by a bus service. Today's Mill Hill East "stub" includes a viaduct over Dollis Road, which holds the record for the highest point at which a tube train travels anywhere on the LU system - sixty feet above ground level !

During this time the LT/LNER interchange station at East Finchley was completely rebuilt under the direction of leading LT architect Charles Holden. It featured a striking statue of an archer pointing towards London, which was designed by the sculptor Eric Aumonier, and which is still in situ to this day. In January 1941, a new low level station was opened at Highgate, directly underneath the existing LNER station. Passengers could change at Highgate, if they so wished, for the branch line to Alexandra Palace. There were plans to electrify this line as well as the section of track northwards from Finsbury Park, through

Highgate, and on to East Finchley. However, the Second World War put an end to these plans as well, and the "Ally Pally" branch remained steam worked until final closure in July 1954.

The High Barnet to Highgate line, as a survivor of the bold expansion plans of the late 1930s, continues to serve a vast travelling public. At the time of writing, the frequency of trains leaving High Barnet for Central London is between three and nine minutes, depending on the time of day, and whether the day in question is in the week or at a weekend. A normal journey to Highgate takes around sixteen minutes, and passengers can be in Central London within half an hour.

High Barnet station still retains its Great Northern Railway (GNR) buildings, which are maintained in good overall condition. The platforms are accessed via the ticket hall and an antique footbridge. Leaving High Barnet, the line gradually curves in an easterly direction, offering views of Chipping Barnet to the right, which includes a glimpse of the Underhill stadium of Barnet Football Club. The first station reached is at Totteridge and Whetstone, which features GNR style brick buildings on both platforms. Woodside Park is the next station along. Once again, the GNR ancestry in the buildings located there are most obvious. A boarded up signal box is located on the "down" platform (in railway terms, the "up" line is that going to London), and a second antique footbridge spans the busy lines. In terms of appearance, the following station at West Finchley is a very different story. It was opened by the LNER in 1933, but was constructed using second hand materials brought from other parts of the LNER system. This was due to the depressed state of the company's finances at that time. This gives the station a very antiquated appearance. However, a recent addition to the station has come in the form of a booking hall on the down platform.

So far in the journey, the character of the area surrounding the line has been semi-rural. However, West Finchley marks a change, with many more buildings to be found on both sides of the line. As mentioned before, Finchley Central, the next station on the line, was known as Finchley Church End. It serves as the interchange for the Mill Hill East branch, which curves in from the right as the station is approached

High Barnet station, during its time as a terminus station of the Great Northern Railway. (Courtesy; RAS Marketing).

from High Barnet. The station itself is of GNR origin (apart from a new waiting room located on the central platform), which contrasts greatly with the classic 1930s style of the next station along, East Finchley. As mentioned above, this locality was an interchange with the LNER branch line to Finsbury Park, and, as a result, it features two spacious island platforms. Leaving here for Highgate, on the left hand side of the line, two tracks can be seen ascending above the Northern Line as it drops down into its tunnel (which for many years was the longest railway tunnel in the world at seventeen miles; it runs as far as Morden in South London). These ascending tracks are all that remains of the Finsbury Park branch. Today this track is used for storage purposes.

At Highgate, the underground station remains something of a 1930s classic, of a type still to be found at various points on the tube network. On going through the ticket barrier and leaving the station by either of the public exits, it is still possible to see the "ghost" station at Highgate High Level, although better views can be gained by using the left hand exit. As mentioned before, this part of the station was on the Alexandra Palace branch. The structure remaining consists of an island platform, with 1930s style tube buildings. With the overhanging trees blotting out much of the overhead sky, the atmosphere is somewhat eerie. It is incredible to believe that such a station still exists in Greater London, over fifty years after the line upon which it was located succumbed to closure.

In conclusion, the High Barnet to Highgate line remains as a good example of what the pre-war LT planners must have hoped to do in the great expansion schemes of the late 1930s - to open up a semi-rural area, encourage people to live outside the City of London, and use their lines as a swift means of commuting to their place of work. It is a function which this particular line has carried out very well to this day, and will continue to do so for many years to come.

THE PIONEER LINE

THE BROXBOURNE TO
HERTFORD EAST BRANCH LINE

The railway line between Broxbourne and Hertford East remains a key part of the tangle of routes that make up the suburban network originating from London's Liverpool Street station more than 160 years after its opening as one of the earliest such routes within the county of Hertfordshire. The very fact that it has been electrified indicates that it will be in use for many years to come.

The seven mile route was originally built and opened for traffic by the Northern and Eastern Railway Company (NERC), the initial date of service being October 31st 1843. It was opened a mere six years after the London and Birmingham line from Euston to Boxmoor and the Midlands, the first railway main line in the world. As with many of the early railway companies, the NERC was taken over by a larger organisation, this being the Great Eastern Railway (GER), which eventually gained control over all of the railway routes beginning at Liverpool Street. For more than one hundred years after opening, the line was faithfully served by steam hauled trains, the locomotives used being either of GER design, or those constructed by the GER's successor, the London and North Eastern Railway. However, in November 1960, the line was electrified, in common with much of the former GER suburban network, and, at the same time, Broxbourne station was rebuilt and re-opened for public use.

The Hertford East branch was the starting point for two other such lines. The first of these was the route from Hertford to Hatfield. This nine mile branch was constructed by another of the early railway companies, the Hertford and Welwyn Junction Railway (HWJR), and was opened for traffic on March 1st 1858. After a series of takeovers and amalgamations, this line came under the control of the Great Northern Railway (GNR) in June 1861. It travelled cross-country from a starting point adjacent to Hertford East (until 1924, when the present day Hertford North station was opened), and passed through the stations of Hertingfordbury and Cole Green, before terminating at Hatfield, thereby providing a useful connection for people who wished to travel to London Kings Cross. Despite early optimism, the line was an early victim of closure, passenger trains ceasing to run in June 1951, less than one hundred years after it was opened. Goods traffic survived for a few years more, although the line was closed in stages, finally fading into history in March 1966.

The second branch line that diverted off the Hertford East route was that between St Margarets and Buntingford. This thirteen and 3/4 mile section was built and opened for traffic by another of the many fledgling companies that sprang up at this time, the Ware, Hadnum, and Buntingford Railway (WHBR). Although the line first came into operation in July 1863, it would seem that there were early financial problems, which culminated in the route becoming part of the GER's empire in September 1868. After passing its centenary, the Buntingford branch was closed to passengers in November 1964 and goods in September 1965.

Happily for both regular customers and railway enthusiasts, the Hertford East branch is still very much in operation, being marketed as part of the "National Express East Anglia" train operating company, who run most of the local and main line passenger trains on the former GER. A typical journey from Broxbourne to Hertford East takes around fifteen minutes to complete. The railway that was constructed by the early pioneers remains the same one that is seen today. The route begins by diverting off the Liverpool Street to Cambridge main line about one mile north of Broxbourne station, this being at Broxbourne Junction. It then proceeds in a westerly direction, surrounded by industrial units on both sides of the line. More houses then appear before Rye House, the first station on the line, is reached. The line is doubled tracked as far as St Margarets, and therefore Rye House boasts two platforms, both of which have modern passenger shelters. On the "up" platform, a single building is in use as a ticket office.

Broxbourne Station looking towards London, and away from the junction with the Hertford East branch 21/7/07. (MJE).

After leaving Rye House, the surrounding area becomes a little more rural in character before arriving at the next station on the line, which is St Margarets. This establishment retains two sizeable platforms, which can accommodate even the longest of the modern electric trains. The station is dominated by a large redundant signal box, which lies at the Hertford end; this being a reminder of the time when St Margarets acted as a junction for the Buntingford branch. A footbridge and level crossing complete the charming scene. A further two mile trip brings the train to the town of Ware, where a single platform and building is located. A second redundant signalbox can be found here, although this is one of a more modern design (most probably being circa 1960s), in contrast to those at St Margarets, and at Hertford East, the terminus of the line.

Hertford East station was constructed by the GER in the 1880s and retains its beauty and elegance. The front of the station dominates the surrounding area, consisting as it does of a large canopy, supported by stone pillars, which provide a welcome for the would-be passenger. Stepping inside the station, the booking hall can be found, and then the station concourse. The two long platforms still retain some of their respective canopies, and the former signalbox stands guard over what remains of the former bay platform and a series of sidings, although these are somewhat overgrown.

The imposing exterior of Hertford East Station 21/7/07. (MJE).

The line is blessed with a good timetable of trains that run between Hertford East and Liverpool Street. At all times, two trains per hour are run in both directions, the journey taking about fifty-five minutes. In conclusion it would seem that things are very healthy for the Hertford East line , and it is to be hoped that this satisfactory state of affairs will continue for a long time to come.

The 17.06 Hertford East-London Liverpool Street local train awaiting departure time 21/7/07. (MJE).

THE RAILWAY THAT NEVER WAS

EDGWARE TO BUSHEY HEATH

It is acknowledged by many transport observers that the present day London Underground Limited (LUL) railway network is one of the most complex of its type in the world. The system has evolved over the course of more than a century, with one of the most intensive periods of development being the years between 1918 and 1939. Hertfordshire benefitted from this expansion of the network with the construction of the Piccadilly Line extension that reached Cockfosters in 1933. Other schemes were proposed but never built, an example being the Edgware to Bushey Heath extension of the Northern Line.

During the first half of the nineteenth century, the Chiltern Hills, that dominate the northern side of London, were a considerable obstacle to the early railway builders. This was because steam locomotives of the day were not very powerful and any gradient encountered had to be made as easy as possible. Although this problem was overcome in time, some towns within the local area had to wait longer than others to be connected to the railway network, one of the dwellings affected being Edgware. At the beginning of the 1860s, Edgware was known mainly as a farming community. As far as the railway network was concerned, the first serious plan that involved Edgware came about during 1861, in the form of a scheme known as the Edgware, Highgate, and London Railway (EHLR). This line was an 8 & 3/4 mile project that would connect Edgware with Finsbury Park and the Great Northern Railway (GNR). The plan was approved by Parliament in June 1862, and construction work began straight away. However, as with many

A scene similar to this would have become commonplace at Bushey Heath had the Underground completed its extension from Edgware. A Northern Line train to London, made up of 1959 built tube stock, pauses at East Finchley in October 1984. (MJE).

early railway companies, financial and commercial type problems were encountered by the EHLR during its short lifetime. Only six months had elapsed since the original approval of the plan when the EHLR was forced to enter into a joint agreement with the GNR. In return for a third of the share capital, and for operating and maintaining the train service on the new line once it had opened, the GNR would take half of the route's gross receipts.

Meanwhile a second local railway scheme was taking shape. Encouraged by the successful passage of the original EHLR Bill through Parliament, a group of landowners drew up a scheme known as the Watford and Edgware Junction Railway Company (WEJRC), and presented a Bill of their own to Parliament in November 1863, the idea being that there would be a junction at the proposed Edgware station with the EHLR. This plan was the first record of any railway scheme linking Edgware with Watford. The short independent life of the EHLR and the WEJRC project came to an end in July 1867, with both company and scheme being absorbed by the GNR. One month later, the Finsbury Park to Edgware route was finally opened for business, and settled down to an unremarkable period of existence that lasted until the arrival of the expanding LUL tube network in the early 1920s.

In the early part of the twentieth century, prior to the First World War, Edgware became the ultimate goal for a rapidly expanding tube line, the Charing Cross, Euston, and Hampstead Railway (CCEHR), which in due course, became a part of the present day Northern Line. By 1907, their tracks had reached Golders Green. Although further work on northbound extensions was stopped during the Great War, once hostilities had ceased, construction recommenced. The line reached Hendon in November 1923, and Edgware became the terminus as early as August 1924. This new Edgware station was a separate one from that of the GNR, which by now had become a part of the London and North Eastern Railway (LNER).From the start of tube running to Edgware, business was very good. Passengers could reach central London in a mere thirty-five minutes, which compared favourably with the sixty minutes of the LNER steam-hauled service, which ran via Kings Cross. Edgware itself expanded rapidly after the arrival of the tube. In 1921, the population had been a mere 1500 people, but by 1939 this had increased to 17000.

In July 1933, the London Passenger Transport Board (LPTB) , which soon became known as London Transport, had come into being, taking over all the underground railway network, with the exception of the Metropolitan Railway, which was absorbed in 1936. Prior to this, in 1935, a five year plan for improving public transport was announced by the Government of the day. Two years later, in 1937, the LPTB presented a Bill to Parliament which was made up of a number of different schemes, one of which was a new extension of the Northern Line, this time from Edgware to Bushey Heath, near Aldenham. As part of the plan, a new railway maintenance depot would be built at Aldenham, to provide extra capacity for Northern Line rolling stock. It was planned that the new line would be worked as a shuttle service from Edgware, with an extra set of platforms to be built there, as a key part of a re-built station. The three mile extension would have had two intermediate stations, these being located at Brockley Hill and Elstree South, before finally terminating at Bushey Heath. This new terminus was to have been located in the triangle formed by the road junction of the present day A41 Watford Way and Elstree Road, which runs to Borehamwood and Barnet, past the edge of the Aldenham Reservoir. Surviving plans for the Bushey Heath terminus show that the new station would have been a grand affair. As well as a car park and bus station, no fewer than forty shops would have been constructed, together with a cinema and a public house.

In July 1937, the LPTB Bill received Royal Assent, work commencing on the new line during October of the same year. At the same time, work began on the building of Aldenham Railway Depot, the aim of these workshops being to provide extra capacity for the storage and maintenance of the rapidly expanding fleet of Northern Line rolling stock. However, events elsewhere ensured that the original plans for Aldenham did not take place.

In 1940, due to the pressures of the Second World War, work stopped on the extension project. However, as Aldenham Depot was nearing completion, it was decided to use the premises as a factory for making aircraft components. From 1941 onwards, it became part of the London Aircraft Production Group (LAPG). This organisation came about as the result of the LPTB joining together with four motor vehicle manufacturers to make parts for the new Handley Page Halifax four-engined bomber, which was coming into front line service with the RAF at that time. Each factory had different components to make. Once completed, the parts would be taken to the final assembly plant, which was at Leavesden Airfield, located near to Watford. The LAPG was so successful that by the time of final victory in 1945, no fewer than 710 Halifaxes (out of a total production run of 6176 aircraft) had been made by the group. As well as the Halifax component section, the De Havilland Aircraft Company built fuselages for their twin engine Mosquito aircraft there, whilst a third organisation, Napier Aero Engines, had a repair and test facility section within the factory premises.

Once peace returned in 1945, and the various aircraft companies left Aldenham, it was assumed that the factory would become a railway workshop, as per the original plan. It was also predicted that the Bushey Heath extension would be completed by 1952. However, the scheme was not awarded as high a priority as other unfinished tube projects, in particular the East- and West-bound extensions of the Central Line. Over the next few years, various reports on the viability of the miscellany of incomplete tube schemes were drawn up by the then new Ministry of Transport and the London Transport Executive (LTE), this latter body being the successor to the LPTB. The conclusion of these various reports and enquiries was that the Bushey Heath extension should not be built.

Since the original building programme had come to an abrupt end in 1940, a number of factors had combined to make the Bushey Heath extension uneconomic to build. Firstly, the arrival of the "Green Belt" scheme would have prevented house building on the scale of the projects that had accompanied LPTB extension programmes of the pre-1939 era. Secondly, the LTE had decided that, instead of using the Aldenham factory for railway work, a small satellite depot would be built at Highgate. This new facility, combined with those that already existed, would cover all the needs of the Northern Line. Finally, the cost of the project was rising steadily. In a report dated 1948, it was stated that £450,000 had already been spent on the extension, and that completion would require a further £1.7 million. The result of all these factors was that the scheme was officially abandoned in February 1954.

This was the end of a fascinating "might-have-been" railway plan. If the scheme had come to fruition, the Bushey Heath extension could have provided a third way into London from Watford, following the national railway route into Euston, and the Metropolitan Line from Cassiobury Park. An extension of the line into central Watford may well have been completed had the Bushey Heath link been opened. However, the downside would have been the creation of a new satellite town to Watford at Bushey Heath, thereby destroying the rural charm of this area. Perhaps this "town" would have looked something like the

If the Underground had reached Bushey Heath, this is the type of train that would have been used on the extension, the "38TS" (this designation being applied to this rolling stock, the first production example of which appeared in 1938). Arguably the finest British tube train ever built, a number of examples are still in everyday service on the Isle of Wight. One of these trains is seen at Ryde Pier Head in 9/2007. (MJE).

The same train seen at Shanklin, the terminus of the "Island Line" from Ryde Pier Head, in 9/2007. (MJE).

immediate area around Rayners Lane station on the Piccadilly Line. The only "winner" from the abandoned scheme was Aldenham, which went on to become the central LTE works for bus overhauls, until its closure in the mid 1980s. At the very least, the end of the scheme ensured that this part of Bushey would remain a quiet backwater and a rural suburb of Watford.

THE FORGOTTEN RAILWAY

WATFORD HIGH STREET TO CROXLEY GREEN

In a separate chapter of this book, the former railway route between Croxley Mill Sidings and Rickmansworth Church Street is described, including its present day role as a public footpath, providing a useful form of recreation for local people. A second line that is perhaps a little better known in the Watford area is that between Watford High Street and Croxley Green. Happily, this section of track is merely "sleeping", looking forward hopefully to the day when it is planned to become part of a flagship Transport for London (TFL) construction project.

The origins of this line are tied in with that of the local suburban railway between Watford Junction and London Euston, known in some quarters as the "New Line" . The original route from Euston to Birmingham was double track only at the time of its opening in the late 1830s, and a third line, this being only for London bound goods traffic, was brought into use during 1858. In 1875, at the culmination of further engineering work, a fourth track was added. At this time, it was decided to build two more lines for local passenger traffic only, these becoming the aforementioned "New Line". This part of the suburban network was finally completed and opened for traffic in February 1913 to a point just short of Watford High Street, forming a junction with the existing Rickmansworth Church Street line. Although electrification of the suburban railway had been discussed as early as 1907, steam traction was employed during its early years. However, in April 1917, electric trains finally started running to Watford on a regular basis, these being provided by the London Electric Railway (which was part of the pre

London Transport tube network), and beginning at Queens Park. The initial service ran on weekdays only; daily running did not start until July 1919, sharing the tracks with the London and North Western Railway's (LNWR) steam service from Broad Street and Euston. A complete LNWR electric service came into operation during July 1922.

A staff line up taken at Croxley Green station. LNWR stands for London and North Western Railway, which means that the picture must have been taken before 1923 (Courtesy; TLOSA)

It was as part of this expanding network that the Croxley Green branch was first constructed, and, as such, was one of the late arrivals on the Hertfordshire railway scene. It was opened for passenger traffic on the 15th of June 1912, and for freight workings during the following October. It began by diverting off the LNWR Watford-Rickmansworth line at a point opposite to where the now defunct railway carriage sheds at Croxley were constructed and opened during April 1917. A new island platform was built at Watford High Street, together with a section of track from the branch onto the Euston line, but facing in the direction of Bushey, thereby creating a "triangle" of lines at this point. The Croxley branch was 2 miles and 54 chains long, and featured one intermediate station at Watford West, together with the terminus at Croxley Green. In October 1982, a third station was opened adjacent to Watford Football Club's Vicarage Road ground, This was called "Watford Stadium", and was used on match days only.

In the early years of the Croxley Green branch, steam power was employed, until it became part of the ever expanding electric network, the first of the new trains coming into service during October 1922. The first type of electric multiple unit (EMU) to be employed were the famous "Oerlikon" sets, a single example of which can still be seen in the National Railway Museum at York. These trains lasted until April 1960, when they were finally replaced by Class 501 EMUs, the newcomers having been built over a period of time beginning in 1957 at Eastleigh Works. These rugged and reliable trains were maintained at the Croxley carriage sheds mentioned before, until they in their turn were taken out of service during the mid 1980s, and succeeded by the Class 313 units, examples of which maintain the present day Watford-Euston service, along with some duties on the Watford-St Albans Abbey line. The demise of the 501s also spelt the end of Croxley carriage sheds, as the replacement trains were looked after at Hornsey Depot, in North London.

The timetable for the line varied considerably over the years. Initially, there were some eighteen trains per day, the majority of which provided a link with Watford Junction; however, some peak hour trains did run to and from the capital. By 1935, the weekday service had improved to three per hour, with a half hour Sunday service. However, the rise of motorised transport affected passenger figures after the conclusion of the Second World War, with all day operation finishing as early as June 1947, whilst Sunday services ceased in 1959. The direct trains to Broad Street stopped running in 1968, by which time a weekday peak hour only service was the norm. This applied for many years until October 1988, when an all day half hour service returned. This new dawn only lasted until January 1990, when the peak hour only service resumed. From mid 1993 to early 1995, the service had become a pale shadow of its former self, with just a single return train running from Watford

Junction, prior to 7.00 each morning ! On numerous occasions, the train was replaced by a bus.

At the time of writing, much of the Croxley Green branch remains in situ, including some of the track. The station platforms at both Watford Stadium and Watford West remain, whilst the remnants of the staircase to the former Croxley Green terminus are still to be found. This part of the line has been isolated for some years, as a new dual carriageway linking the Croxley Business Park with the main Watford to Rickmansworth road has cut through part of the former embankment. It should be emphasised that, although the line is disused, the land upon which it is situated remains railway property and should not be trespassed on by members of the public. Despite appearances to the contrary, the line is still legally open.

What of the future ? A scheme which has been spoken of for many years is a plan to link the Croxley Green branch, via a new section of railway, to the Metropolitan Line of London Underground, at a point between Watford Met and Croxley stations. At the present moment in time, Hertfordshire County Council (HCC) and London Underground Limited (LUL), along with a host of other interested parties, are looking to bring the dream of a "Croxley Rail Link" into being. The idea is to run Met trains direct into Watford Junction, with a new station being built at Ascot Road (this being to serve the industrial estate), and the former Watford West station to be refurbished. A double track line would be laid as far as Watford High Street, where further upgrading work would be carried out. The present tube terminus at Watford Met would be closed as a result, and it is hoped to run Metropolitan services to Baker Street from Watford Junction as often as every ten minutes. In 2004, the capital cost of the scheme was estimated to be around £65 million. Transport for London (TFL) has pledged a substantial contribution towards this cost, whilst it is hoped that all or part of the remainder will be provided from central government. If all goes to plan, it is hoped to bring the link into public service in a period of between five to seven years.

After having spent the majority of its life as something of a railway backwater, it is a fascinating prospect for the Croxley Green branch to perhaps end up as part of the London Underground network. Time will tell as to whether the Croxley Rail Link comes to fruition; however, the completion of this bold plan would ensure the long term future of the line.

RAILWAY WALKS

The remains of Lemsford Road station, located between Nast Hyde and Hatfield, on the GNR branch line to St Albans 18/8/07. (MJE).

A WALK ALONG
THE NICKEY LINE

THE FORMER BRANCH LINE BETWEEN
HARPENDEN AND HEMEL HEMPSTEAD

Although it is more than 25 years since the last working section of the former Midland Railway (MR) branch line between Harpenden and Hemel Hempstead was closed and the track lifted, there are still some items of railway interest that can be found on a walk along the old trackbed. Much of the line has been converted into a public footpath which is called, fittingly, the "Nicky Way" (for some reason, the "e" in "Nickey" has been deleted). The scheme was set up as the result of a joint effort between various local councils, and other organisations, including a support group, the "Friends of the Nicky Line", contact details for which can be found on notice boards located all along the line. The footpath was originally opened for public use in December 1985, and is a credit to everyone concerned. Thanks to the efforts of the various groups involved, a 7.5 mile section of footpath can be used, and it is quite easy to imagine trains passing through the lush Hertfordshire countryside.

The original branch began at Harpenden Junction, just north of Harpenden station on the Midland main line from London St Pancras. The left hand cutting into which the old line ran immediately after leaving the main route can still be seen clearly, although fencing has been built at this point to separate the footpath from the working railway. A long flight of stairs descend from street level to the start of the "Nicky Way", and some items of railway interest can be found at this point. The most notable is a brick retaining wall, to the left of the former cutting, together with an MR built brick bridge, which carries a minor road over the footpath. Looking back through this bridge, it is possible to see the course of where the original connection to the MR main line was made; this connection curved away in a left hand direction.

The first stop on the line after leaving Harpenden was at Roundwood Halt. It is remarkable that, even though passenger services were withdrawn from the line as long ago as June 1947, part of this tiny station is still in situ. The remains are made up of part of the single platform, together with a replica "distant" type semaphore signal, both items standing at the Hemel end of the station. The remainder of the platform has been buried under some earthworks that have been built up to enable people to join or leave the footpath from nearby housing estates. Both signal and platform serve as a reminder of times past, and are a bonus for the railway enthusiast.

On leaving Roundwood Halt, the "Nicky Way" leaves Harpenden behind, and makes its way into open countryside, the footpath gradually descending as it nears Redbourn. Just before reaching the site of the old

Roundwood Halt, looking towards Harpenden. The halt is guarded by a replica distant semaphore signal 2/6/07. (MJE).

The remains of Roundwood Halt, the first station along the line from Harpenden. This view is taken looking towards Hemel Hempstead 2/6/07. (MJE).

Redbourn station, the built up embankment upon which the original line was built has been broken by the construction of the Redbourn by-pass. Nature has reclaimed the site where the old station was built, and the casual traveller would not know that such an establishment ever existed. The footpath continues alongside the bypass, before ascending, in order to cross the A5 trunk road by way of a well maintained bridge. This is followed immediately by a second bridge, which crosses the River Ver, a river which has come back to life in recent times after a period of years as nothing more than a dried up river bed.

At the time of writing (which was in June 2007), the footpath was broken at this point by various road works mainly being undertaken in conjunction with the widening of the nearby M1 motorway. Visitors to the footpath need to leave, and descend via a second footpath to the old Redbourn road, which runs parallel to the former railway line. The "Nicky Way" can be re-joined on the far side of the motorway bridge,

Redbourn station circa 1920. Note the small goods yard to the right of the picture. (Courtesy; The Lens of Sutton Association (TLOSA)).

at a point opposite that of the hotel that is located there. The junction where the old Redbourn road meets the by-pass is also the site of the next station on the former line which was known as Beaumont's Halt. As at Redbourn, no trace remains of either the station or its adjacent building.

The next section of the walk, on the Cupid Green side of the motorway bridge, is the most rural on all the route, and it is hard to believe that the industrial area of Hemel Hempstead is less than two miles away. After the various railway artefacts to be found at the Harpenden end of the line, this part of the walk is devoid of such curios, although the remains of a gradient post can be found at Woodend Lane bridge, another MR brick-built structure. The footpath is now approaching the site of where the Hemelite Concrete premises were located (the goods trains that were run from here to Harpenden Junction were the reason for the former line remaining active for so long after the end of British Railways traffic). This site has now been filled by various warehouses. Two further bridges are to be found at this point, one a road bridge that carries the footpath over

Nickey Line information board located at Cupid Green 2/6/07. (MJE).

a minor route which connects the B487 Hemel to Redbourn road with one side of the Maylands Avenue industrial estate. This is followed by a much narrower bridge which has been installed since the line's closure, and which crosses what was the entrance to the former Hemelite factory. This was also the point at which an engine shed had been located; this building housed the two diesel locomotives that were used by Hemelite to work their goods trains.

Beyond the footbridge, the "Nicky Walk" ends somewhat suddenly in the industrial area built up around Eastman Way. To access the next part of the walk, it is necessary to follow Eastman Way as far as a rubbish dump, where more signposts can be found, directing the would-be walker to the next part of the footpath. All signs of the former trackbed have been lost at this point, and the next time that it can be traced is to the rear of the main Ford garage situated on Redbourn Road. The re-development of the surrounding area has erased all traces of the next station on the line at Godwins Halt, another single platform station of a type similar to that at Roundwood Halt. Leaving behind Redbourn Road, the walk re-commences and descends towards the bridge spanning the Queensway road, which itself runs from Cupid Green to central Hemel Hempstead. The gradient at this point was 1 in 40, which was a severe struggle for Harpenden bound trains. The steep nature of the path at this point gives an indication of how tough their task must have been. The Queensway bridge itself looks as much a permanent feature of the local landscape as the day that it was built, and is a familiar landmark to people using the road to drive into and out of Hemel.

Beyond the bridge, the old trackbed has once again been lost to housing development. Using a footpath through the local park, it is possible to regain it at the other side of the housing estate and follow it up as far as the main road at this point, which is known as Midland Road. Here the railway bridge has been filled in with earthworks, and all traces of the original Hemel Hempstead station, which was located on the other side of the bridge, have been lost to housing. However, a reminder of the old line can be seen in the form of the "Midland" public house, which is located at this point - a welcome sight for thirsty walkers! On the 100th Anniversary of the line's opening in 1977, a plaque was installed in the pub to mark this major milestone.

Beyond the "Midland" public house, much of the former route of the line has been lost to development over the period of time that the New Town of Hemel Hempstead has been in situ. Hemel Hempstead station itself has been submerged under a combination of both houses and small industrial units, although, at the time of writing, these units have become redundant, and are to be demolished, with the land utilised for more housing. However, it is possible to judge where the line ran by looking at the top of the former bridge on the opposite side of the main road at this point.

It is possible to follow an adjacent course to that of the former line by taking the next left hand turn along the main road, this being Mayflower Crescent, and then taking a right-hand fork into Caernarvon Close. A footpath between two of the houses on the right hand side of this road leads into a cul-de-sac, known as "The Sidings", a small reminder of the goods yard that was situated at the old station. Straight ahead at this

Hemel Hempstead station circa 1914. The building in the left hand background is now the Midland public house. The bridge in the right hand background is now the starting point of the Nickey Line walk. (Courtesy; TLOSA).

point, a t-junction can be seen, at which a left hand turn should be made into Alexandra Road. The railway ran parallel to the latter part of this road, crossed Hillfield Road, and continued behind West Herts Hospital and the Marlowes shopping centre. It is possible to continue walking a parallel course to the former trackbed, by carrying on down Hillfield Road, taking a left hand turn into King Harry Street, and accessing a left hand footpath, which terminates in Maynard Road. This latter road continues along the back of some modern offices. In times past, the railway swung right to cross the Plough roundabout by means of a viaduct, which was closed and demolished in 1959. In the wake of the development carried out as part of the building of the New Town, all traces of this impressive structure have vanished. For the determined walker and railway historian, a plan of action would be to access Cotterells by means of walking along Selden Hill and Moor End Road, and then crossing Leighton Buzzard Road via a pedestrian crossing.

The site of where the railway ran through Cotterells has been obliterated by the construction, during the early 1970s, of the skyscraper building that was used by Kodak for much of its life. From here, the line ran adjacent to the present day pitch belonging to the local cricket club. At the back of the pitch lies the Grand Union Canal, and the remains of one of the supports belonging to the bridge that took the line into the common land that lies beyond the Canal are still visible. This stretch of land contains the largest surviving section of this part of the line, in the form of an embankment, together with three former railway sleepers, and the retaining walls of one half of the bridge that took the route over the former A41 London Road, and onto Boxmoor Gasworks, into which much coal traffic was taken for most of the railway's existence. Beyond the old A41, once again, all traces of the line have been lost, this time to purely industrial development. However, by following the footpath along this road in the direction of the present day Hemel Hempstead

Heath Park Halt circa 1907. The train standing at the station consists of a former Midland and Great Northern 4-4-0 tank locomotive, plus a single Pullman car built by the Midland Railway towards the end of the 19th Century. (Courtesy; TLOSA).

railway station, and by accessing a left hand turn, Roughdown Road, it is possible to cross the main line to the south of Hemel station, and to see where the short lived connection between the Nickey Line and the main line was situated by looking to the right in the direction of Hemel. A closer view of the same point can be gained by walking to the Hemel station carpark, and looking from its far end.

In conclusion, more of the line's trackbed has been saved than might otherwise have been the case, bearing in mind that the bulk of the original route was closed during the early 1960s. The "Nicky Way" footpath is a credit to those who created it, and those who look after it. It enables current and future generations to see conclusive proof that a Harpenden to Hemel Hempstead railway really did once exist

THE ST ALBANS
RAILWAY WALK

THE FORMER GNR ST ALBANS
ABBEY–HATFIELD BRANCH LINE

All over Britain, many of the lines that were closed as part of the railway modernisation plans of the 1950s and 1960s have found new leases of life as public footpaths or cyclepaths. An outstanding local example of this enlightened policy can be found in the conversion of the former branch line between St Albans Abbey and Hatfield.

"Alban Way" signpost, situated near to St Albans Abbey station 12/7/07.
(MJE).

The origins of this particular railway line lie in the construction of the first stage of what is now the main route between London Kings Cross and Edinburgh Waverley. In 1850, the then fledgling Great Northern Railway (GNR) opened up their new line between Maiden Lane (this establishment being located adjacent to the site of the present day Kings Cross station) and Hatfield, and then on to Peterborough. It was quickly realised by the GNR that a potentially large source of revenue could be gained by connecting Hatfield to the city of St Albans by means of a horse-drawn bus service. This service was initiated and, for a while, the GNR enjoyed a monopoly of St Albans traffic. This state of affairs continued until 1858 when the rival London and North Western Railway (LNWR) constructed and opened its branch line to St Albans Abbey from Watford Junction. The GNR realised that drastic action would have to be taken if it were to retain even a slice of the St Albans traffic. The company decided to form an independent railway company for the purpose of building and operating a new branch line between Hatfield and St Albans Abbey. In June 1862, the Hatfield and St Albans Railway Company (HSARC) was incorporated by an Act of Parliament. Construction of the new route commenced at once, although trains did not begin running until October 1865. In the early years after the line's opening, the amount of traffic generated was not as much as had been hoped. After some years of financial struggle, the HSARC was taken over by the GNR in 1883. After the 1923 railway "grouping", the GNR became part of the London and North Eastern Railway (LNER), which in turn became British Railways (BR) upon nationalisation in 1948.

Despite the best efforts of both the GNR and the LNER, passenger and freight traffic remained at a low level. In particular, the amount of passenger revenue during the 1920s and 1930s fell to such depths that the LNER decided to withdraw the service upon the outbreak of the Second World War in September 1939. However, in a strange twist of fate, the service was re-introduced in December of the same year because of the large numbers of people who used the trains in order to get to their place of work at the De Havilland aircraft factory, this being located at Hatfield. These employees mainly used the halts at

Nast Hyde and Lemsford Road to get to and from their place of work. Following the end of the war in 1945, passenger traffic returned to its former low level, and the whole service was finally withdrawn by BR in September 1951. As with many such lines, goods traffic soldiered on for a few years, general traffic lasting until September 1964. After this, trains were run on an "as and when" basis. In 1967 the track between St Albans Abbey and Butterwick Sidings (between Smallford and Hill End) was lifted, whilst the remainder of the line to Hatfield was closed in December 1968.

As mentioned previously, much of the trackbed has been converted into a public footpath. A typical walk might well begin at St Albans Abbey station, one platform of which is still in service, being used by the electric multiple units that travel over the 6.5 mile former LNWR route to Watford Junction. The bay platform that was used by the Hatfield trains is still in situ, with much of the vegetation that took over the trackbed at this point in recent years having been tidied up as part of the general upgrading of the whole station. The best way of accessing the walk is to turn right upon exiting the station, and taking the next right hand turn, known as Prospect Road. At the far end of this road, a footpath on the right hand side leads to the start of the walk (which is known at this point as the "Alban Way"), the point of which is marked by the bridge which carries Cotton Mill Lane over the former trackbed. The distance from here to Hatfield varies between five and six miles depending upon which roadsign is read !

After walking in the direction of Hatfield for a short while, a housing estate is reached. In a pleasant surprise for both the railway enthusiast and the general observer, the station building for St Albans (London Road) is still very much in situ. Both building and platform have been cleaned up, and the building itself now has a modern day function as an office block. It is incredible to think that such an unusual structure has not only survived, being located near to the city centre, but can pay its own way at the same time. Food for thought for other such buildings located around the country? After leaving this station, the path passes under London Road itself by means of a bridge. Until recently, it was still possible to note a pair of steam age smoke deflectors fitted to the underside of the bridge, although these have now vanished. Immediately ahead at this point, it is possible to see the massive brick viaducts that were built by the Midland Railway (MR) in order to carry its main line to London St Pancras, these huge structures being constructed in the latter part of the 19th century.

The former London Road station buildings, now used as offices 12/7/07. (MJF).

The next point of interest on the line is the overgrown platform that is located on the left-hand side of the path a short walk on from the MR viaducts. This was formerly Sanders Siding and Halt. This station was opened in the mid 1890s to serve Sanders Seeds Merchants, the premises of which were located adjacent to the station. This business carried on until the early 1950s when the company moved away from St Albans. It is very easy to miss seeing the old platform, so great is the amount of vegetation that has grown all around and over it in recent years. Further along the line, the next siding was located at Camp Road.

The former station building at St Albans (London Road), viewed in 1999. The station itself was located one stop along from St Albans Abbey on the GNR branch to Hatfield. In an enlightened piece of restoration, the building is now converted for use as a company office. (MJE).

This was named Salvation Army Siding, due to the nearby location of the Salvation Army Printing Works. At the time of the line's closure, the original bridge was demolished, although a new bridge has been constructed in more recent times, thus enabling footpath visitors to cross above Camp Road, rather than having to descend to road level, as was previously the case.

Between Camp Road and Sutton Road, the path skirts the rear of the supermarket located at Fleetville. It then continues along for a short distance before it becomes necessary to descend to road level. This is in order to cross Sutton Road, the reason for the descent being the demolition of the bridge that was in situ. After crossing Sutton Road, the original trackbed can be regained via a small drive, which is located adjacent to the former Fleetville sidings. Previously, this area was the site of a travel company, where coaches of various types were stored,

A 1950s view of St Albans (London Road), the photographer standing at right angles to the main road of the same name. (Courtesy; RAS Marketing).

Salvation Army halt. The fact that the note on the photograph mentions the London and North Eastern Railway (LNER) indicates that the picture was taken some time between 1923 and 1948. (Courtesy; RAS Marketing).

although it has now become a housing estate. At one time it was believed that a weighbridge was buried in the former approach road.

Leaving Sutton Road, the path continues onwards, passing underneath Ashley Road by means of a 1960s built concrete bridge, and then it passes through into more open countryside. Hill End Station is the next landmark on the line, the old platform still existing alongside an estate made up of mobile homes which now occupy the rest of the site. The next major point of railway interest during this part of the walk is the bridge that was constructed in 1930 to carry Colney Heath Lane over the railway. At this point, on the left hand side of the walk, many industrial warehouses have been constructed, these continuing to the site of the next station on the line, which is at Smallford. The station building survives to this day, although it is surrounded by other structures, including a portacabin, and covered by vegetation. In addition, the platform still exists, as does a bridge, which carries Station Road over the former trackbed.

The somewhat eerie remains of Hill End station platform. Beyond the fence is a site for mobile homes 12/7/07. (MJE).

Following Smallford, the most rural part of the walk is reached. This continues for about a mile or so until the former Nast Hyde Halt is reached. As with Sanders Siding, Hill End, and Smallford, it is possible to miss the platform that is still located there, covered as it is by vegetation. Leaving Nast Hyde, the next section of the walk passes through a housing estate. It is still possible to trace the course of the line when leaving the estate, as it continues under a further road bridge, this carrying Comet Way into Hatfield. Following the bridge, the next part of the former trackbed has been swept away by the widening of the A1 (M) road from London to the North. The path itself turns left at this point and concludes at a location opposite to the Galleria shopping centre.

"Alban Way" signpost at Nast Hyde, just outside Hatfield 12/7/07. (MJE).

The walk continues on the far side of the dual carriageway that runs in front of the Galleria shopping centre. An underpass connects the two parts of the Alban Way, and the footpath continues down the right hand side of the Galleria. The path is entirely surrounded by houses on both sides at this point. After crossing Lemsford Road, another gem can be found in the form of the platform used at the former Lemsford Road Halt. However, prior to the building of this small station, a siding had been installed at this point in 1880 for the benefit of local businesses, and it had been extended in 1894. The siding became known as Fiddle Bridge, due to the nearby location of an inn of the same name. The Halt itself was opened in August 1942 for the benefit of employees of the nearby De Havilland Company's aircraft factory. It was felt by all concerned that the provision of such a halt would make it easier for people to get to and from their place of work. It was also thought that if people used the train, rather than drive their cars (although this would have applied to only a small number of workers), it would not give away the location of the factory to German aircraft, as a number of cars parked together would have done.

The platform remains are overgrown by many years' worth of vegetation. However, it is still somewhat surprising to find them here, surrounded as they are by developed areas of land. Leaving Lemsford Road Halt, both Wellfield Road and Homestead Road are crossed, following which the line dives into a cutting. The end of the walk is soon reached, and the path concludes in a side street. A footbridge located straight ahead takes the pedestrian across the main railway route between London Kings Cross and the North. Looking to the right from the bridge, Hatfield station itself can be seen. The original line from St Albans joined the main line via a set of points facing towards London, although today all traces of this have vanished beneath new housing, whilst Hatfield station itself was reorganised during the electrification of the then Eastern Region suburban network during the 1970s. From the bridge, it is but a short walk along the Great North Road back to the station itself.

In conclusion, the Alban Way (or Smallford Trail, depending on whereabouts the walk is either joined or left), serves not only as a useful form of recreation for many people, but also as a reminder of a long lost railway route, It is to be hoped that its current tidy state will be maintained in the years ahead.

THE EBURY WAY WALK

THE FORMER WATFORD TO
RICKMANSWORTH RAILWAY

In recent years, Hertfordshire has benefitted from the enlightened policy of converting the trackbeds of old railway lines into public footpaths. Two obvious examples are the "Nicky Way" from Hemel Hempstead to Harpenden, and the "Alban Way" which takes in the old route from St Albans Abbey to Hatfield. Watford is also lucky in this respect and is served by the "Ebury Way", a four mile footpath, which connects West Watford to Rickmansworth. The walk utilises the trackbed of the former railway line that ran from Croxley Mill Sidings to Rickmansworth Church Street.

The "Ebury Way" walk began its railway life as part of the branch line that ran from Watford Junction to Rickmansworth. This route was the brainchild of Mr Robert Grosvenor, the third son of the Marquis of Westminster. Mr Grosvenor was the MP for Middlesex from 1847 to 1857, whereupon he was made Lord Ebury. The original plan was to connect Rickmansworth to Watford, where the main London to Birmingham line (the first of its kind in the world) had been constructed and opened for traffic during the late 1830s. In July 1860, the Royal Assent was obtained for the building of the new branch, and, in November 1860, Lord Ebury himself turned the first sod at Rickmansworth. Construction was brisk, and the new 4.5 mile line was opened to the public in October 1862. The name of the company that was responsible for building the new route was the Watford, Rickmansworth, and Uxbridge Railway (WRUR). Even at this early moment in time, Lord Ebury had ambitious plans for his new railway. In 1861, he had looked to obtain Parliamentary permission to extend the still uncompleted Watford-Rickmansworth section onto Uxbridge, from where a connection with the Great Western Railway (GWR) was to be made. It has been suggested that the ultimate aim of this scheme was to build a cross-country line from Uxbridge to Hertford. However, as with many schemes put forward in the early days of the "Railway Mania", lack of available capital meant that the Watford-Rickmansworth section was the only part that was completed.

After opening, the line was operated by the London and North Western Railway (LNWR) on behalf of the WRUR until 1881, when the LNWR purchased the route outright. The branch led a fairly orthodox existence over many years, the only major events taking place firstly in 1923, when the LNWR was taken over by the London Midland and Scottish Railway (LMSR), which in its turn became part of the British Railways system upon nationalisation in 1948. Prior to this, in September 1927, the line was electrified by the LMSR, although steam locomotives were still responsible for the freight traffic that made its way along the branch. As part of the goods services provided, various sidings were built for the benefit of larger companies whose premises were located along the branch; these included Benskins Brewery and John Dickinson's paper mills, based at Croxley.

Despite the electrification programme of the late 1920s, passenger traffic was eroded by local bus competition and the rise in private car ownership. It was no surprise when these trains were withdrawn in March 1952. Freight traffic was a little luckier; this survived until 1967, when the services run west of Croxley Mills to Rickmansworth were discontinued and the track lifted. The final part of the line, from its junction with the route from Watford High Street to Croxley Green, to the Dickinson sidings at Croxley Mill was closed in 1983 and the remaining trackwork lifted soon after.

The present day "Ebury Walk" can be accessed from many points along its route, although a logical point to start would be at Bushey & Oxhey railway station. On alighting from one of the numerous local services, it is necessary to take the Pinner Road exit, turn left to walk under Bushey Arches, cross over Eastbury Road, and then into Lower

High Street. Immediately on the left can be found a footpath which enters Colne Valley Linear Park; this path continues through the park, under the rail viaduct (which carries the local line between Bushey and Watford High Street), alongside the River Colne, and onto Wiggenhall Road. After crossing this road, the start of the Ebury Way proper can be accessed by walking left for a few yards, where the local recreation ground can be found; this being located to the right of Wiggenhall Road. A footpath is provided in order to cross the ground; this eventually joins up with Riverside Road, which is a residential area. At this point, a view of Watford Football Club's Vicarage Road ground can be found above the trees seen to the right. Beyond here, the footpath leaves the course of the road, and bends first right, then left, through a playground, from where it bends right once again. At this point, it changes from a made up to an unmade footpath. A few yards further on, the former railway trackbed is accessed via an embankment.

From this point, up until the start of the Moor Park industrial estate,

The former railway bridge that spanned the Grand Union Canal, near to the outskirts of Watford, and now part of the Ebury Way 7/7/07. (MJE).

open countryside can be seen to the left, whilst glimpses of West Watford can be found to the right. There are few railway relics to be found along the walk; however, the remains of a gradient post can be seen to the left of the footpath, whilst a large brick bridge, of railway origin, is used to cross over a canal. Within this part of the walk, the former trackbed begins on an embankment, but then dips into cuttings of various depths, until the bridge underneath Tolpits Lane is reached. The aforementioned Moor Park industrial estate can be found on both sides of the path beyond the bridge, the modern hi-tech buildings looking somewhat out-of-place in this semi-rural location. Moor Lane crossing is the next point of interest on the walk, and, beyond this, Croxley Common Moor can be found. The industrial estate gradually fades away, the final buildings located where the bridge carrying both London Underground and Chiltern Railways trains cross over, the silence being punctuated at regular intervals by train sounds, which seems somewhat strange walking along an old trackbed which has not seen a train of its own for some forty years!

An Ebury Way signpost at Croxley Moor 7/7/07. (MJE).

Passing underneath the railway bridge, the most rural part of the walk can be found, with various lakes and reservoirs being seen on both sides of the path. The Grand Union Canal (GUC) is crossed a little further on, and this point is possibly the most scenic in all the walk. Looking from the footpath bridge to the right, it is possible to see the River Gade divert from the canal via a right hand fork, a lock just beyond this river junction, and in the background, the Underground/Chiltern joint railway line is seen once again. Beyond the canal bridge, over-hanging trees tend to block out much of the light, the path becoming narrower at the same time. A final item of railway interest can be found at this point to the left of the path; this being a complete gradient post. The end of the walk is now in sight, with the GUC re-appearing to the left of the path. Many narrow boats can be seen tied up at this point.

The appearance of a housing estate here marks the end of the Ebury Walk. The footpath itself comes out on the main road joining Rickmansworth town centre with the roundabout for places such as

A remarkable survivor of the old railway. A redundant gradient post near Rickmansworth on the Ebury Way 7/7/07. (MJE).

Northwood, and at a point nearly opposite to Rickmansworth Church. The local canal museum can be found within the course of a very short walk; instead of turning right for the town, potential visitors should bear left, and across the roundabout, whereupon the museum can be accessed via a descending flight of left hand side steps. A good time to visit the museum would be on the occasion of the Canal Festival; this is usually held over a weekend during the month of May.

The housing estate here was built on the site of the former Rickmansworth Church Street station. Looking at the site today, it is very hard to imagine that a railway was ever located here, although the walk provides evidence otherwise. In summing up, the Ebury Walk provides a source of recreation and exercise for many local people. It also serves as a reminder of another local railway line that has perished in the face of more modern forms of transport.

A CROSS-COUNTRY LINE

THE HERTFORD TO HATFIELD
BRANCH LINE

Within the sprawl of lines that form the suburban network beginning at London's Kings Cross station, Hatfield is seen as one of the larger towns to be found, serving a wide area with a considerable population. On today's modern railway, it is merely a "through" station, located as it is on the East Coast Main Line. However, in times past, Hatfield was the starting point for no less than three branch lines. Two of which, the routes to St Albans, and to Dunstable and Luton, are featured elsewhere within the covers of this book. The third line, the subject of this chapter, was the nine mile route to Hertford, which was one of the earliest lines to be built within the locality.

The origins of this line began with the formation of a company known as the Hertford and Welwyn Junction Railway. This organisation was the outcome of a group of businessmen from both London and Hertford coming together to promote their scheme for a Hatfield to Hertford link. The project gained Parliamentary approval in July 1854, although it later became involved with a second scheme which evolved into the line that was constructed between Hatfield, Luton, and Dunstable. The two groups were merged together and collectively became known as the Hertford, Luton and Dunstable Railway (HLDR), the idea being to construct a cross-country line to join up three of the major routes, these being the Midland, Great Northern, and Eastern Counties Railway (which later became the Great Eastern). The new company was approved by a second Act of Parliament in June 1858. Politics were also at work; there was a fight going on between the Eastern Counties and Great Northern

Railways for the traffic that was being generated by the county town of Hertford. In 1861, this particular dispute was partially solved by the Great Northern taking over the HLDR.

Prior to this date, on the 1st of March 1858, the line between Hatfield and Hertford was opened for public use. As previously mentioned, it was a nine mile route, with just two intermediate stations, these being located at Hertingfordbury and Cole Green. Hertford itself already had a station, Hertford East, served by the Northern & Eastern Railway, which had been built as far back as 1843. The terminus of the HLDR branch was located at Cowbridge, roughly half a mile west of the existing establishment. At Hatfield, the branch ran parallel to the existing GNR main line, as it was not allowed to cross the major route. It then turned towards Hertford at a point near to Welwyn. At first no station was provided here until 1920, when a single platform was constructed. It was not until 1926 before something bigger was built ; this co-inciding with the start of what became known as Welwyn Garden City, complete with its large industrial area, the most famous residents of which were Nabisco (the makers of "Shredded Wheat" breakfast cereal) and the Murphy Radio organisation.

The building of the GNR's Hertford loop line during the early part of the twentieth century had a great impact on the Hatfield to Hertford branch as it led to the construction of a new terminus at Hertford. The origins of the loop came about because the GNR wished to increase line capacity at the London end of the East Coast Main Line (ECML), but it wanted to avoid the major expense that would be involved in building additional trackwork. It therefore decided to construct a "loop" line, Parliamentary approval being given in 1898. The GNR had earlier built a line to Enfield that was completed in 1871. The loop was formed by running the new line from Enfield to Stevenage. Progress was very slow in constructing the link, but eventually the line reached Stevenage in 1920, and it is a route that is very much in use today, as part of the electrified suburban network. One of the stations built along the line was that at Hertford North, and it was decided that the Hatfield line should terminate there, rather than at Cowbridge. There was, however, a further delay in starting passenger services on the loop line, these not commencing until the 2nd of June 1924. From the same day, Cowbridge was closed, and branch line trains utilised the new station instead.

During the course of its life, the branch did not generate the traffic levels that its promoters had hoped for. People that lived in Hertford preferred to travel to London from Hertford East, via Broxbourne, to Liverpool Street. This train service was much more frequent than that on the branch. The beginning of the end came in 1939 with the start of the Second World War. During 1944, the London and North Eastern Railway (LNER), which had absorbed the GNR at the Railway Grouping of 1923, built a direct connection between the branch and the main line at Welwyn. From this time onwards, branch line trains terminated here instead of at Hatfield. Even this radical re-shaping of the passenger service did not stop the decline in revenue. It was decided to close the line to passenger trains, and this sad event took place on the 18th of June 1951. Goods trains carried on for a few more years; however, these too

A "Cole Green Way" sign, located at the Hertingfordbury end of the walk 2/9/07. (MJE)

were withdrawn during May 1966.

Happily, the majority of the trackbed has remained in situ to this day, having become part of the "Cole Green Way", which in its entirety is a ten mile route linking Ware, Hertford, and Welwyn Garden City. A good place to start the railway part of the walk is at Hertford North station. Leaving the station exit, a right turn along North Road should be made, until the junction with Hertingfordbury Road is arrived at, this being after a walk of some ten to fifteen minutes. The latter road should be crossed over at this point, whereupon a further fifteen minute stroll brings potential walkers to a right hand turning, West Street. After a few minutes walk, this road forks left; it is at this point that the Cole Green Way begins, the footpath being well sign-posted. To begin with, the path takes a somewhat meandering course around one side of the ground belonging to Hertford Town Football Club. It is here that the old trackbed is accessed, and the path goes underneath the viaduct that carries the Hertford Loop line on its southward journey to Enfield and onto the capital. This viaduct is a magnificent structure and worthy of closer attention whilst passing beneath it.

After leaving the viaduct, the old trackbed dives into a deep cutting that is somewhat overgrown. It is here also that a slight gradient begins, one that continues past the former Hertingfordbury station. This establishment has now been converted to a domestic residence, and a fence has been constructed along the old platform for privacy purposes. However, it is quite easy to spot the railway origins by looking at the roofs of the building in question. The platform edges can also be picked out quite easily. From looking at old pictures of the same station, it is very noticeable that nature has reclaimed much of the ground around the station, with many trees overhanging the building, giving the whole scene a somewhat melancholy atmosphere. Beyond Hertingfordbury, the former trackbed continues to climb through a mixture of both cuttings and embankments. Hertford has been left behind by now, and the surrounding area is very much a rural one.

For the railway enthusiast, there is not too much of the old infrastructure left on this line between the two former stations at Hertingfordbury and

The viaduct at Hertford North, carrying the "Hertford Loop" line, connecting Stevenage with Enfield, and ultimately, London Kings Cross. The Cole Green Way continues under the viaduct on the extreme left hand side of this picture 2/9/07. (MJE)

Cole Green, other than a bridge that spans a road leading into the hamlet of Birch Green, and many different types of concrete posts, either for fences or crossing gates. However, at Cole Green itself, both platforms are still in situ. Although that on the left hand side is overgrown by vegetation, its opposite number on the right has been converted to serve as a small car park, complete with wooden posts along the platform edge to prevent unwary motorists driving their cars too far! A picnic area and a public house can be found here, and it is a useful place to both join and/or leave the walk. One can sit here on a quiet day and imagine that a slow branch line train will soon be arriving.

Upon leaving Cole Green, the trees that have grown up on both sides of the old line, blotting out some of the sunlight, gradually disappear, and open fields are found instead. The distant roar of road traffic indicates the adjacent A414 trunk route, which the footpath negotiates by way of a

Cole Green station. The platform opposite the one shown is still in situ 2/9/07. (MJE)

The overbridge at the Hatfield end of Cole Green station, which carries the trackbed over a minor road 2/9/07. (MJE)

modern underpass. The footpath then follows a winding course, running almost parallel to the B195 Cole Green Lane, a route which crosses the A414 in the course of its journey, and ends up in the village of Cole Green itself. Eventually, footpath and road meet, this being the end of the Cole Green Way. For the determined walker, however, it is possible, by following the appropriate blue signage, to take a more or less straight route as far as the centre of Welwyn Garden City itself. Unfortunately, the old trackbed is lost beyond Cole Green Lane, much of it having fallen victim to the considerable development that has taken place in the locality over many years.

In looking to sum up the history of the Hertford to Hatfield line, it is possible to suggest that, like many other railways all over the country, it was built as a competitor to a nearby rival, rather than to serve an obvious transport need. Much of this unnecessary situation arose as the result of railway politics and infighting that took place during the years of considerable building, this period of time spanning much of the nineteenth century. Such lines were easy victims of the road transport revolution that took place following the end of the Second World War, and formed the bulk of those routes cut down during the 1950s and 1960s. At least this particular line is still partly in situ as part of the public footpath network.

FROM COUNTY TO COUNTY

THE HATFIELD, LUTON
AND DUNSTABLE RAILWAY

Elsewhere within the covers of this book, I have described two of the railway lines that helped to achieve the aim of a cross country route between Leighton Buzzard and Hertford, these routes being those that ran between Leighton Buzzard and Dunstable, and Hatfield to Hertford. In this chapter, I will describe the middle section of this link, namely the branch line that ran between Hatfield to Luton and Dunstable.

The history of this line goes back almost to the dawn of railways in 1846, when the young Great Northern Railway (GNR) proposed a branch line to Luton, mainly as a counter-proposal to plans by the rival London and North Western Railway (LNWR) to construct a route from its main line at Leighton Buzzard to Dunstable, which was completed and brought into use during 1848. In 1851, the National Census of that year revealed that Luton had the dubious honour of being the largest town in Britain to have neither rail nor canal transport links. At this moment in history, 16,000 people lived in Luton, and local industry had grown to the point where no less than £2m worth of goods were being manufactured every year. Clearly the unfavourable transport situation was one that needed to be rectified and as soon as possible. At this time, businessmen living in Luton had petitioned the LNWR to extend their Dunstable branch into Luton, but without success. A similar approach was made to the GNR, but with the same result. In time, however, the combination of local businessmen and landowners, together with other dignitaries, such as the MP for Hertford, combined to promote a scheme which became known as the Luton, Dunstable, and Welwyn Junction

Railway Company. This ambitious plan called for a line beginning at Dunstable, running through Luton, and on to Welwyn, where not only was a junction to be made with the GNR's main line between London Kings Cross and the north, but a bridge would have crossed the GNR to make direct contact with the branch between Welwyn and Hertford, where a further connection with the Northern & Eastern Railway (NER) would be made.

In yet another example of the railway politics that could be-devil plans and projects of this particular moment in time, the GNR was hostile to the idea of a bridge spanning its main line in order to connect the two branch lines. In a somewhat wasteful use of money, men and materials, both companies were forced to run tracks parallel to the GNR main line from Welwyn to Hatfield, a distance of some three miles. This additional work no doubt contributed to the financial problems which befell the promoters of the Dunstable-Welwyn scheme, and, as a means of raising the necessary capital, they joined with the company building the Hertford branch, the Hertford and Welwyn Junction Railway. The joining together of the two groups had the added advantage of pooling other resources as well. In spite of opposition from some quarters, the plan worked, as not only did the Hatfield-Hertford line begin running in 1858, but the first section of the Luton line, between there and Dunstable, opened to goods in April of the same year, whilst passenger services commenced the following month. The final stretch of the line between Luton and Hatfield opened for business in September 1860.

The line was a single track one, just over twenty miles long. Passing loops were provided at three of the stations along the route, these being at Ayot, Harpenden East, and Luton Bute Street. In the beginning, the LNWR worked the section between Dunstable and Luton from April 1858 to August 1860, when the GNR took over responsibility for the whole line through to Dunstable. The initial section of the line, from Welwyn to Luton, was of a very rural nature, passing through arguably some of the finest countryside in both Hertfordshire and Bedfordshire. After leaving Welwyn, the line passed through Ayot, which served the nearby villages of Ayot St Peter and Ayot St Lawrence. The next station on the line was the charming hamlet of Wheathampsted, before passing through Harpenden East (this being a separate station from that serving the Midland Railway), Luton Hoo, and then into Luton Bute Street.

It was here that the line became more "industrial" in character, which of course was part of the idea for building it in the first place. Between the two Luton stations, the line paralleled the Midland Railway (MR) main line, and, just prior to arriving at Bute Street, for many years ran adjacent to Vauxhall Motors, which was the jewel in the crown of Luton's industrial might. Leaving Luton, the branch then ran in a north-west direction towards Chaul End Halt, before terminating at Dunstable Town, a station that was more convenient for the town centre than the LNWR station at Dunstable North.

The early years of the line were good ones. As early as 1864, the GNR was providing a daily service of seven trains between Hatfield and Dunstable, with six in the opposite direction. By 1900, these figures had become nine and eight respectively, with the LNWR thoughtfully providing seven connecting services between Dunstable North and Leighton Buzzard. From the start of the twentieth century, for a period of some fifty years, the line settled down to a steady and unspectacular existence, not unlike many similar routes all over Britain. As yet, there was very little competition from internal combustion vehicles, and the railway had a near monopoly of land transport. From the railway enthusiast's point of view, a solid variety of steam locomotives could be found on the branch, beginning with a cross-section of both tank and tender locomotives, designed by two of the foremost Chief Mechanical Engineers (CMEs) of the GNR, these being Mr Archibald Sturrock and Mr Patrick Stirling, the latter also responsible for the GNR's premier express locomotives in the 1870s, the "Stirling Singles", these being one of the most beautiful of all British steam locomotives ever built, with their eight foot diameter pair of driving wheels. A single example exists to this day, and can be found in the National Railway Museum at York. From the 1920s onwards, more modern and powerful tank engines could be found hard at work on the branch, on a mixture of both passenger and goods trains. These were of the N1, N2 and N7 types, the two latter being designed by the CME for much of the life of the London and North Eastern Railway (LNER), Sir Nigel Gresley. Sir Nigel later designed the A4 streamlined express passenger locomotives, one of which, "Mallard", still holds the world speed record for steam traction.

By 1945, the line had survived the deprivation and hardship of the Second World War, and was still offering its passengers a daily service of some seven trains between Hatfield and Dunstable, with nine being run in the opposite direction. However, during the 1950s, the effects of car, lorry and bus competition were starting to be felt. Diesel locomotives of various types took over running the train services from the old steamers in a bid to cut costs - however, this bold plan was not successful, and, after many years of steady decline, the passenger service was withdrawn in April 1965. In contrast, freight traffic was still plentiful along certain sections of the line, these being between Luton and Dunstable, and Hatfield and Blackbridge Sidings, which were situated near Ayot. Ayot itself had lost its station buildings as the result of a somewhat unfortunate fire in July 1948, the station then being closed to passengers in September the following year.

As time went past, even these small pockets of activity diminished, the Blackbridge Sidings to Hatfield freight workings coming to an end in May 1971, and the final section, that between Dunstable and Luton, seeing its last train as late as 1988. Oil and chemical trains had been the staple diet of this section, being run for the benefit of the oil storage depot based within Dunstable. After this, the tracks remained in situ until 1994, although British Rail (BR) had officially closed the line two years earlier in 1992.

Elsewhere within this book, I described a walk along a separate part of this line, that being between Luton Hoo and Harpenden East. However, there is a second part of this line that provides a latter day function as a public footpath, this covering the section between Welwyn Garden City (WGC) and Wheathampsted, and being known as the "Ayot Way". This path can be accessed via a set of footsteps descending from Digswell Road, WGC, these being located to the rear of the city's public library at Campus West. An ornamental bridge takes Digswell Road over the

An "Ayot Greenway" sign, seen between Ayot and Wheathampsted 9/9/07.
(MJE)

footpath, and a left hand turn should be made at the bottom of the steps; this leads out of the city and into Sherrardspark Woods, a very rural setting in complete contrast to the large shopping centre only recently left behind. The old trackbed climbs steadily, before emerging from the woods at the B197 Great North Road. The footpath can be accessed on the far side of this road by turning into Ayot Green, which leads to the delightful village of the same name, after crossing over the busy A1M trunk road. The path has temporarily left the course of the old railway whilst passing through the village; it regains it via the entrance to the former Ayot station driveway, which now leads to a car park. The former trackbed now finds itself upon an embankment which can be clearly seen from the road.

From here, the Ayot Way runs more or less in a straight line over the three miles to Wheathampstead, the total mileage for the hike from Welwyn Garden City being six in all. Throughout this section the trackbed finds itself in a mixture of both cuttings and embankments,

The remains of Ayot station, located between Welwyn Garden City and Wheathampsted on the Hatfield to Dunstable branch line 9/9/07. (MJE)

with the gradients being a gentle mixture of both uphill and down. Two fine examples of railway bridges can be found, one spanning a footpath, whilst an overbridge located near Waterend Lane carries a similar walkway high above the old line. Approaching Wheathampstead itself, the path bends sharp left, finishing in the delightfully rural Sheepcote Lane. From here, it is possible to take a half hour walk that brings visitors to the centre of Wheathampstead itself, via Marford Road, and the High Street. For the railway enthusiast, the greatest piece of hidden treasure is saved until last. On the far side of the town, where the High Street joins the B653 road between Harpenden and Luton, a large part of the single platform can still be found, covered in vegetation, and isolated on its own piece of embankment. The railings at the back of the platform are still in situ, and it is still possible to trace where the track went, looking in the direction of Luton, although the bridge that spanned a side road has been demolished and houses have been built across the course of the track.

In conclusion, the Hatfield, Luton and Dunstable line has quite obviously been consigned to the dusty pages of history, its trade taken away by more modern means of transport. However, the two footpaths located along different parts of its route ensure that it will live on, providing a link with the past.

GREAT EASTERN MEMORY

THE BUNTINGFORD TO
ST MARGARETS BRANCH LINE

In a separate chapter within this book, I describe the branch line between Hertford East and Broxbourne, a route which is still very much in use, having found its niche as part of the suburban railway network originating from London's Liverpool Street station. However, for many years, there was a second branch line that began at St Margarets, one of the intermediate stations along the Hertford East branch. This route ran to the market town of Buntingford, almost on the Hertfordshire/Essex border.

At the beginning of the 19th century, Buntingford had become a thriving market town. The main reason for this was that it was situated very near to the Great North Road, which today has become the A1 trunk route, and, as a result, the town was in a very good position to gain passing trade. However, this position was changed by the coming of the railways. Whilst many centres of population benefitted from being linked to the new method of transport, Buntingford found itself in a somewhat isolated position, being bypassed by both the Eastern Counties Railway's main line between London and Cambridge, and also by the trunk route of the Great Northern Railway, this latter line connecting London to Hitchin, and the North. Clearly, such a situation was not acceptable to the town. On the 1st of August 1856, a meeting of local landowners, businessmen, and other interested parties was held at a hostelry located within Buntingford, this being the "George and Dragon" hotel. The purpose of this gathering was to propose the building of a railway line from Buntingford to the Northern & Eastern

Railway (NER) at Ware, this being the second intermediate station on the Hertford East branch. The plan was a response to the failure of an abortive scheme to construct a route between Ware and Cambridge, which would have taken in Buntingford.

The general plan was agreed by all present at both this and a subsequent meeting held later that same year. A company was formed to bring the plan to fruition, the scheme becoming known as the Ware, Hadham, and Buntingford Railway (WHBR). An application was made to Parliament in November 1857, and the Act to build the new route was passed on the 12th of July 1858. The building of the line was fraught with difficulties, which commenced even before the turning of the first sod in July 1859. A group of landowners objected to the line being joined to the NER at Ware. Therefore, it was decided to locate the junction with the Hertford East route at St Margarets, this station being located nearer to the Broxbourne end of the line. During the building of the branch, much compensation was paid to owners of plots of land across which the new line was built. Such problems threw a considerable financial strain on the fledgling WHBR, to the extent that the nearby Eastern Counties Railway (ECR) had to invest the not inconsiderable sum of some £22,000 in the scheme in order to aid completion. The thirteen and three quarter mile line took almost four years to complete, during which a second Act of Parliament was passed in 1862 for an extension to the original building time estimated three years earlier. A bridge that crossed the line at Braughing, one of the intermediate stations, was failed by a Board of Trade inspection even before the line was built. The offending item had to be re-built prior to the official opening, which took place on the 3rd of July 1863.

Although, prior to the opening of the line, the WHBR had entered into an agreement with the ECR to operate and maintain the new railway, by the time that the opening day arrived the ECR was no longer a separate company, having become part of the Great Eastern Railway (GER) in 1862. Although the GER took over the working arrangements agreed between the WHBR and the ECR, relations were somewhat fraught on both sides. The WHBR considered the facilities offered by the GER

*Ex-London and North Eastern Railway (LNER) N7 0-6-2 tank locomotive
69688 at St Margaret's station on a Buntingford bound train 4/4/1959.
(Courtesy; B.W.L.Brooksbank/Initial Photographics).*

inadequate, whilst the bigger organisation thought its share of the route's receipts too little to meet the cost of operating the line. This unfortunate turn of events was brought to an end in September 1868, when the GER purchased the line. Despite these problems, the line itself had got off to a successful start. As well as Braughing, five more intermediate stations had been built, these being located at Westmill, Standon, Hadham, Widford, and Mardock. It has been suggested that this last named establishment derived its name from a nearby farm known as Mallocks Farm (although it is now known as Marlocks Farm). In the early timetables, the station was known as Mardocks. The line itself was single track, with passing loops. In the beginning, there were four trains in each direction on weekdays, with half that number on Sundays, the journey time being forty minutes. In the first six months, some 30,000 passengers were carried on the line, but goods traffic figures were very discouraging, mainly due to the lack of suitable goods sheds and sidings along the branch. A derailment at Buntingford became the catalyst for the GER to improve and upgrade the trackwork, whilst the early station buildings were demolished and replaced by more modern structures.

At the start of the twentieth century, the line entered upon the period of its greatest success. Residential areas had been built up, this process being aided by the outward growth of the London suburbia, the result being increased revenue for the branch. Even the somewhat erratic amount of goods traffic had been expanded to the point where three trains per day were run prior to the start of the Great War in 1914. As a contrast, the daily passenger service at this time had been expanded to eleven in each direction, this including a through train from Buntingford to London Liverpool Street. The commuter traffic was supplemented by leisure traffic, in particular walkers and ramblers, keen to explore the surrounding area. In fact, the line gained a well-deserved reputation as one of the most scenic within the locality.

In 1923, the railway "Grouping" meant that the miscellany of private railway companies were merged into one of four large groups. For the Buntingford branch, this meant that it now became part of the London and North Eastern Railway (LNER), the successors to the GER. By this time, some trains were running in both directions between London Liverpool Street and Buntingford. However, a cloud appeared during January 1924, in the form of a seven day rail strike. As a result, many passengers were lost to the line, never to return, which upset the receipts as a result. It could be said that the decline of the route began at this time, although, during the Second World War, the siting of an ordnance depot at Buntingford provided much extra freight traffic.

As with so many similar lines, a more rapid downturn in passenger and freight began at the end of the war in 1945. Although modern diesel multiple unit (DMU) trains had replaced the steam hauled stock in 1959, increasing private car ownership made the line's future uncertain. Passenger habits were also changing; people preferred to drive to nearby stations with a direct service to the capital, rather than use the branch and change at St Margarets. Buntingford's own direct service to London was withdrawn at the end of the 1950s, and many off-peak services went the same way. At this time, the only bright spots for the line were a

*Ex-LNER N7 69693 departs from St Margarets station on a Hertford East-
Liverpool Street working 4/4/1959.
(Courtesy; B.W.L.Brooksbank/Initial Photographics).*

combination of film location work, and testing of prototype rail vehicles,
these normally then being sent for export. The publication of Doctor
Richard Beeching's "Re-Shaping of British Railways" report in 1961
sealed the fate of the branch, as it did with so many other lines. By 1963,
a mere two thousand passengers per week were using the line. Closure
proposals were implemented by British Railways (BR) at this time, and
despite a vigorous campaign to save the branch by local people, the
final passenger train ran on the 14th of November 1964. Somewhat
surprisingly, freight traffic outlasted its passenger counterpart by almost
a year, the final goods train running to Buntingford in September 1965,
although a short section of track from St Margarets to a nearby gravel pit
remained in operation until March 1969.

Despite the passage of more than forty years since it was closed,
traces of the branch can still be found. At Buntingford itself, the station

building is still in situ. In the past, it was used as office space by a local engineering company. However, it is currently empty, with broken windows seeming to emphasise the somewhat melancholy air which surrounds it. Although the trackbed at this point has been lost to a more recent housing development, a nearby public house has a railway theme for its name, providing a reminder that a railway did once run to the town. As for the rest of the branch's trackbed, some sections survive as public footpaths, although others have been incorporated into the improved A10 trunk road between London and Cambridge. However, Braughing station is still very much in situ. The station building has become a private residence, whilst both platforms have been preserved, together with a signal box and the small wooden establishment located on the platform opposite to the main building. A reproduction semaphore signal still guards the entrance to the station at the St Margarets end, whilst a single railway coach has been located on an isolated piece of

The station building at the former Buntingford station, depicted in April 2002. At the time, it was in use as offices, but is now redundant. (MJE).

track. Period signage completes a remarkable piece of restoration, and credit must go to all concerned.

The relics that remain at both Buntingford and Braughing, together with the other traces of the line that are still to be found, serve as a reminder of a long forgotten route, one that could be seen as an LNER answer to "Metroland", attracting people to live along its length, and then using the route to commute to their places of work in London. However, its remote location made it an easy victim of the post war private car revolution, along with many other similar lines. Today it lives on only in the printed word, or within the hearts and minds of long term local residents.

The former station building at Buntingford, now sadly out of use 22/9/07.
(MJE)

PRESERVATION

A miniature replica of a "Britannia" class locomotive 70026 "Polar Star". It is seen at the Tyttenhanger Light Railway in October 2007 being prepared for a new journey. (MJE).

MAGIC IN MINIATURE

THE NORTH LONDON SOCIETY OF MODEL ENGINEERS AND THE TYTTENHANGER LIGHT RAILWAY

It is pleasing to report, even in times where much of the engineering section of British industry has been lost for various reasons, that the model engineering hobby remains strong and active throughout the country, with many clubs and private individuals continuing to "fly the flag", by constructing and operating a wide cross-section of items. One of the most active organisations within the area covered by this book is the North London Society of Model Engineers (NLSME). A glance at their website shows that the group caters for many different modellers and subjects, with a host of active sub-sections making up the whole that is the NLSME.

The NLSME was originally formed as long ago as 1944. More than sixty years on, it still adheres to the aim upon which it was originally founded, this being "to promote and encourage model engineering, and its related pastimes". Although the purpose of this particular chapter is to focus on the railway-related activities within the Club, other modes of transport are also catered for, within a number of the different sub-sections. One of these is known as the "Marine Section", and, as can be guessed from its title, caters for those interested in building and operating model boats. The headquarters of the NLMSE are located at Finchley, where the members of the marine section meet on a regular basis during the winter months. In the summer, both members and private individuals are encouraged to visit the section's very own boating lake at Colney Heath. This is open on both the first Sunday afternoon and the third Friday evening of each month, the duration of each season being from Easter to

The imposing station sign on the "raised railway" at the North London Society of Model Engineers' Colney Heath site, this being one of no less than three circuits of track, catering for live steam and modern traction locomotives of various gauges 7/10/07. (MJE)

Halloween. A second non-railway section of the NLSME is that catering for slot-cars of various types. This is known as the "Slot Car Section", and meets every Thursday in a specially prepared clubroom at Finchley. Both newcomers and those already familiar with the hobby are catered for. A Club shop enables both cars and spares to be purchased, whilst a separate championship for Scalextric vehicles are held at Finchley on alternate Fridays. What is re-assuring is that help is available for people wishing to improve their knowledge and understanding of their chosen subject.

The largest division within the NSLME is the "Locomotive Section", this group catering for members whose main interest lies in the construction and operation of live railway locomotives. This section utilises the Society's outdoor site at Colney Heath, which is located near to St Albans. No fewer than three separate circuits of track have been built, all of which can accommodate locomotives of different gauges. The longest of these three circuits is that known as the "Mainline" track, which has been built upon a raised concrete structure. This line caters for engines of both 3.25" and 5" gauge, whilst the neighbouring "Cuckoo Line" is used for those locos of 2.5", 3.5", and 5" gauge. Finally, the ground level circuit looks after engines of 7.25" and 5" gauge. The site is open to the public every Sunday afternoon from Easter to the end of October, between 2 and 5pm. It is possible, at any time, to see a considerable cross-section of locomotives, both steam and modern traction. These engines are normally a mixture of freelance designs and faithful replicas of many of the classic locomotives of years gone by.

A visit to the Colney Heath site (or the Tyttenhanger Light Railway (TLR), to give it its proper title) is a fascinating experience, and one that can be most rewarding for attendees, whether they be families, casual passers-by, or railway enthusiasts. Model makers will find much to interest them. The TLR is located in Church Lane, Colney Heath, and is situated to one side of a water pumping station. Prior to entering the car park, visitors are immediately made aware that they are entering a railway environment, by the presence of a level crossing, which takes them over the ground level railway. On arriving at the site, the Locomotive Section's workshops are the first point of contact. Here, visitors can observe the engines being prepared at close quarters, on specially raised sections of railway. It is also possible to talk with the owners of these fascinating machines, discovering all manner of information. On the circuits themselves, rides are given behind these engines, thus enabling people to see them hard at work, demonstrating their comprehensive haulage capacity. On the raised railway, it is interesting to note that the whole line is protected by fully operational colour light signals, thereby enabling more than one train to be operated at busy times. Members of the NLSME are always on hand, ready to answer any questions that visitors may care to put to them.

The railway atmosphere at the TLR is enhanced by the addition of various artifacts, including semaphore signals and former station lamps. The centre of the site has been marked by the construction of a replica

An example of a live steam locomotive, being prepared for work at Colney Heath. This engine is a replica of a Great Western Railway 2-6-0 mixed traffic locomotive of the 43XX class 7/10/07. (MJE)

platform, complete with an old fashioned type canopy. Tables and chairs are provided for those wishing to make use of the buffet-bar, this being situated within an old parcels coach that has been grounded (this is a railway term, for rolling stock without wheels). One half of the coach acts as the buffet, whilst the other has been converted into a mess room for use by Society members. From here, visitors can keep an eye on what is going on, whilst enjoying something from the considerable selection of food and drink on sale (the former including delicious home-made cakes). All profits from the sale of these refreshments go to the Society, thus enabling more improvements to be made on the TLR. At the time of writing, an extension was planned to be added to the "raised" railway, enabling it to be run to the rear of the waterpumping station.

To sum up, a visit to the TLR is a worthwhile experience. The atmosphere is very laid-back, and yet much can be seen in action. It can almost be described as a further extension of the railway preservation movement, bringing to life miniature replicas of locomotives from the past, the original prototypes of which have long been scrapped. It is a quiet location, providing a welcome refuge from the hustle and bustle of the outside world. Best of all, visitors are making a positive contribution towards the ongoing success of a worthy and long-lived organisation - the NLSME.

Website: www.nlsme.co.uk

FOR THE ENTHUSIAST

A replica headboard used by the St Albans Locomotive Club of Great Britain seen in July 1990. (Courtesy of Barry Smith).

107

THE ST ALBANS BRANCH OF THE LOCOMOTIVE CLUB OF GREAT BRITAIN

A SHORT HISTORY

In the fifty odd years since the beginning of the plan to preserve the narrow gauge Talyllyn Railway in North Wales (the world's first such scheme), Britain has become the leader in this field, with many fine preserved railways and museums located all over the country. However, the county of Hertfordshire is, unfortunately, without a heritage railway, although miniature railways, such as the North London Model Engineering Society's base at Colney Heath help to satisfy the locally based steam starved enthusiast. At a more "grass roots" level, there are a number of railway clubs in different parts of the county, organising talks and lectures of various kinds. One of the most active groups in this field is the St Albans Branch of the Locomotive Club of Great Britain (LCGB).

The St Albans LCGB first came into being during May 1963, and, for the first season only, joint meetings were held at the Midland Railway Hotel in St Albans (this public house now known as the Horn of Plenty), with the local branch of the Railway Correspondence and Travel Society (RCTS). The very first talk given to the joint branch was a colour slide show organised by Mr A. Sutcliffe; this taking place on the 23rd of July 1963. By May 1964 nine talks had been held on various subjects, with the branch having the bonus of making a small profit of £2. 2s 0d on the year's activities. Meetings continued during the winter months of the following few years; however, in 1967 the RCTS involvement in the group ceased and it became an LCGB branch only.

During those early days of the branch, the policy of arranging sales

A Branch visit to the then Network South East Aylesbury Depot (this is now part of Chiltern Railways), during October 1992. The diesel train seen sustained damage by being charged by a bull during its previous journey! (Courtesy of Barry Smith).

stands at local railway events began with an appearance at a traction engine rally at Elstree in 1968. This policy has remained a useful source of both publicity and revenue for the branch, and it is one that continues to the present day. During the same year the first ever outdoor visit took place, this being to the two signalboxes at St Albans City station. The North side box has since been demolished, but the South side is still very much in situ, currently being restored by a separate voluntary group of enthusiasts. The steady expansion of branch activities continued during 1970, when on October 17th of that year, the first "Claydales" railtour took place, running between Hemel Hempstead and Redbourn on the "Nickey Line" during the time when it was operated by the Hemelite Concrete Company. The sixty participants had a problem at the start of the journey - no wagons were available for them to travel in ! In a move which would cause present day Health and Safety officials sleepless nights, it was decided to split the party into three groups of twenty. Within these groups, eight travelled in the cab of the Hemelite diesel shunting locomotive used, and two groups of six clung to the handrail on each side of the engine. Despite these happenings, the three round trips to Redbourn were completed without any mishaps. Photographs of the event appeared in the national "Railway Magazine" and local newspapers, including the now defunct "Evening Echo". This outing was the forerunner of three similar trips, run at various dates up to 1975.

Since those early pioneering days, the branch has grown into one of the most active within the LCGB. This is due to the efforts of many people, in particular those past and present members of the Branch Committee. In 1980, the branch moved its meeting place to its present day location at the United Reformed Church in Chiswell Green. This appears to be a popular choice with both members and visitors, as the attendances have remained at a healthy level. At the time of writing, the average monthly attendance for the 2006-7 season was more than fifty people. The branch is very lucky in this respect, having a good core of members who come to the meetings on a regular basis, while a generous sprinkling of visitors come along to talks covering a particular topic, a good example of this being a lecture in February 2005 by railway author Peter Tatlow on the aftermath of the infamous 1952 Harrow and Wealdstone train accident, when an above average attendance of more than ninety people was attained.

A healthy programme of outdoor visits to various places of railway interest are carried out; these range from walks along abandoned lines to block bookings on railtours. As mentioned before, sales/publicity stands are set up at local model exhibitions and toyfairs, whilst a comprehensive publicity effort is arranged on behalf of the branch. This consists of programme mailshots, mobile publicity displays at places such as libraries, and even broadcasts on local radio stations! Four editions of the branch newsletter are issued during the course of a typical season (such a season runs between September and May), keeping members and visitors alike in touch with what is happening within the branch.

A Branch visit to the Waterloo and City line of London Underground, prior to its rebuilding, also in 1992. Members are seen in the signal cabin at Bank. (Courtesy of Barry Smith).

It also complements the information found in the LCGB's own house magazine "The Bulletin". The branch even has its own page on the official LCGB website, thus helping to spread "the word" even further. The branch committee of seven people work very hard overseeing all this activity and there are other members of the branch who are willing to help out with activities such as sales stand duties and supporting the outdoor events.

The branch marked its 40th Anniversary in October 2003 with a special dining car trip on the preserved Great Central Railway (GCR), running between Loughborough and Leicester North, the steam locomotive in charge being one of the only two original GCR tender locomotives still in existence today, this being 2-8-0 freight locomotive 63601. A special touch was provided by an LCGB headboard being placed on the front of the engine, whilst the menu included (appropriately enough) steam pudding! A nice touch to round off a splendid day.

For the future, the branch is looking to maintain its current active status. Further details of meetings can be obtained, either by contacting the branch secretary on 01727-861839, or by accessing the LCGB website on; **www.lcgb.org.uk.**

BUCKINGHAMSHIRE

Bletchley in April 1999, with the Bedford service being made up of two "Bubblecar" type heritage DMU's. (MJE).

NATIONAL RAILWAY SYSTEM

A Marlow bound train sits in the platform at Bourne End 30/6/07. (MJE).

A THAMES BRANCH LINE

MAIDENHEAD-BOURNE END-MARLOW

Over the last fifty years or so, many areas of Britain have been shorn of the numerous branch lines that once criss-crossed the landscape. One such area is that covering parts of Buckinghamshire and Berkshire, within the territory of the former Great Western Railway (GWR) and its famous main line from London Paddington to Wales and the West Country. There are but few survivors of a once extensive network of lines in this area. However, one such route that has managed to defy this somewhat depressing trend is that from Maidenhead to Marlow, via Bourne End.

The present day Maidenhead to Bourne End line had its origins in a scheme authorised by Parliament as far back as 1846, which called for the construction of a 5.5 mile route between High Wycombe and Bourne End. This scheme evolved into a more ambitious High Wycombe-Maidenhead project, the latter section of which became the line that is still in use today, running via Cookham and Furze Platt. Although this line was constructed by the independent Wycombe Railway Company (WRC), it was worked by the GWR, who later absorbed the WRC in 1867. Three years later, in 1870, in common with what was happening on the rest of the GWR system, the line was converted from the "broad gauge" of 7ft 0.25" to the standard gauge (common to the rest of the British railway network) of 4ft 8.5".

Until the early part of the twentieth century, the line settled down to an uneventful existence, providing the starting point for many a journey for people living in the local area. There was also a steady flow of freight traffic at this time. However, in 1906, the GWR, in partnership with the Great Central Railway (GCR), completed the last part of a joint section of main line that passed from the Midlands, through High Wycombe and Beaconsfield, and into London Paddington. This was a quicker and more direct route into the capital (and vice versa), than the High Wycombe to Maidenhead line, and soon passenger numbers on the latter route began to fall away, although the line retained a nucleus of traffic and was an important link between the two GWR main lines.

The story of the Bourne End to Marlow branch began with its opening to traffic in 1873. Marlow itself had been by-passed by the early "Railway Mania" era of the mid-nineteenth century. This was despite being situated a mere thirty miles from London. Eventually, a scheme was drawn up for a two mile branch line, which formed the basis of the route that runs to this day. It was constructed by yet another of the early independent railway companies, the Great Marlow Railway (GMR), and it followed the course of the River Thames to a spacious terminus on the eastern side of Marlow. As with the High Wycombe-Bourne End-Maidenhead line, its operation was carried out by the GWR, and, as with the WRC, the GMR was eventually absorbed into Paddington's empire in 1897.

In the early days, the bulk of the traffic to be found on the Marlow-Bourne End line was provided by the commuters who lived in Marlow and the surrounding area, although some freight traffic was also to be had. Steam power worked the line until July 1962 when the all conquering diesel multiple unit (DMU) was introduced in its place.

The modern day Maidenhead-Bourne End-Marlow line remains very much in operation as a part of the First Great Western (FGW) franchise. The vast majority of customers would most probably begin their journeys at Maidenhead station's platform five, from where the branch line trains depart. A charming overall roof not only provides welcome shelter for branch passengers, but adds a warm glow of nostalgia. In fact it can be said that Maidenhead station is something of a throwback to the days of steam, for while the Marlow train can be found at a separate bay platform, connecting with the FGW suburban trains to London and the

"Networker" DMU 165119 is seen in the bay platform at Maidenhead,
awaiting departure time for Bourne End. Maidenhead station is lucky as it
still retains overhead canopies on both platforms 30/6/07. (MJE).

West, the express railway can also be found, with the evergreen High
Speed Trains rushing through the station to their various destinations.

Leaving Maidenhead, the line swings sharp right, away from the main
line, and onto an embankment, beneath an overbridge, and into a cutting.
Houses can be found on both sides of the line, before Furze Platt, the first
station on the branch, is reached. This establishment consists of a single
platform, and what appears to be a small booking office. The station
also marks the boundary between the edge of Maidenhead and the open
countryside beyond. Leaving Furze Platt, it is not long before the next
station at Cookham is reached. Here, the working single platform is in
stark contrast to the defunct platform opposite, which was the location
of a passing loop. An unexpected bonus for the railway enthusiast is
the fact that the station building on the defunct platform is still in situ,
having become part of an office complex. On departure from Cookham,
it is but a short while before the outskirts of Bourne End are reached.

The line swings sharp right, crosses the River Thames by way of an attractive three span girder bridge, and arrives at Bourne End station itself. The line to Marlow can be seen on the left at this point, joining the original route just prior to the conclusion of the train's four mile journey from Maidenhead. The section of track beyond Bourne End to High Wycombe was closed in May 1970 due to falling traffic receipts, and the station at Bourne End has been modified to fit its new role as a terminus. The former bay platform that accommodated the Marlow train in steam days has vanished under a series of industrial warehouses, whilst the long canopy that was to be found on this platform has been demolished, along with the footbridge. However, the GWR style ticket office is still very much in operation, and some historic buildings can be found on the opposite side of the station to the warehouses, one of which serves as an auction room.

After a pause of around five minutes, which enables the crew to change ends, the train is on its way once again, this time bound for Marlow. On leaving Bourne End, the line curves sharply to the right, being hemmed in by houses on both sides. After it straightens out, the line begins to run parallel with the Thames, which can now be found on the left hand side of the train.

After a scenic journey of around two miles, the increasing amounts of houses and industrial units which can be found on both sides of the line signify the approach of Marlow and the terminus of the line. Marlow station is a shadow of its former self, consisting of a single platform, which is located in the goods yard area of the original station. This was closed in 1967, and the ground has been used for another industrial development. However, a pleasant reminder of the days of steam can be found in the form of the "Marlow Donkey" public house, which is located opposite the roadway to the station, this strange name being that bestowed upon the line during the steam era. The phrase "Marlow Donkey" originally came from a nickname for the horses and mules that pulled barges along the Thames at this point, prior to the coming of the railway.

The Maidenhead-Bourne End-Marlow branch line has settled well

Bourne End station 30/6/07. The line to Maidenhead swings away to the left of the picture, whilst those to Marlow sweep away to the right. (MJE).

The 17.06 Marlow-Bourne End train, seen at Marlow, awaiting departure time 30/6/07. (MJE).

into its role as a vital component of the FGW suburban network. The train frequency is a good one, services running on an hourly basis all the time, apart from a half hour timetable during peak hours only. However, the gentle pace of the journey, and the rural nature of parts of the line, evoke memories of an earlier age, providing interest for both the railway enthusiast and the seasoned traveller.

RAILWAY WALKS

The former Verney Junction station. A line of track can be made out in the centre foreground 19/8/07. (MJE)

MADE IN BRITAIN

THE CHEDDINGTON TO
AYLESBURY BRANCH LINE

Within the twenty thousand route miles of railways that used to criss-cross the British landscape, one of the most fondly remembered features was the country branch line, in many cases a piece of single track, connecting remote hamlets to a part of the main line system. Often, the locomotives used were those that had been superseded by more modern types, and, in the days of steam, the train itself would be made up of ancient coaching stock, and even, in some cases, would be a mixed formation of both passengers and freight. Some branch lines still exist at various places around the country, having survived the mass closure programmes of the post-1945 era. It is interesting to note that the first of these many branch lines to be built in Britain was the otherwise unremarkable seven mile section of track between Cheddington and Aylesbury.

The origins of the Cheddington to Aylesbury line are tied in with those of the pioneering London and Birmingham Railway (L & BR), the world's first railway main line. Construction of this large undertaking began in June 1834, and by September 1838 the whole route had been completed. Various interested parties within the town of Aylesbury took note of what was happening with the new railway, and, in November 1835, a scheme was proposed to link Aylesbury to the new line. One of the branch line's most staunch supporters was Sir Harry Verney, a prominent local landowner, and later MP for Buckingham, who was helpful in enabling the new scheme (which by now was known as the Aylesbury Railway) to obtain an Act of Parliament, this major event occuring in May 1836. Construction did not begin for a further two years; this was in order to await the outcome of a separate scheme to build a new line between Aylesbury and Cheltenham. However, as with many of the early schemes, this venture came to nothing, and work on the branch commenced under the leadership of none other than Robert Stephenson, the son of George Stephenson, and an extremely capable engineer in his own right.

Cheddington station, looking towards London, July 2000. (MJE).

The line began at Cheddington. As the steam locomotives of the day were very under-powered, the route was straight and had only very slight gradients. There was but a single intermediate station built, this being at Marston Gate, almost half way between Cheddington and Aylesbury. The line was opened for public use on 10th of June 1839, and, during the early period of operation, all locomotives and rolling stock were supplied by the L & BR. At this same time, traffic levels were not as high as the line's proposers had hoped; however it managed to gain a foothold within the local economy. In 1846, the L& BR was taken over by the London and North Western Railway (LNWR), which meant that the Aylesbury route passed into new ownership as well. The LNWR was the result of an amalgamation of several of the early railway companies, including the Grand Junction, the Liverpool to Manchester (the world's first railway line to be opened specifically for passenger traffic), and the Manchester to Birmingham. As a result of this take-over, LNWR motive power began to appear on the Aylesbury route, and revenue began to increase. As mentioned before, there was but one intermediate station on the branch, this being located at Marston Gate, which was a distance of 2 & 3/4 miles from Cheddington. It originally opened in 1857, primarily as a goods station. It catered for local milk, cattle, manure, and other types of farm traffic.

From the opening of the line until the early 1860s, its owners, in particular the LNWR, were able to hold a monopoly of Aylesbury traffic, due to it being the only railway in the area. This was in spite of a number of alternative schemes, all of which came to nothing. However, the Great Western Railway (GWR) was in the process of expanding its broad gauge empire from Paddington, and in October 1863, the Wycombe Railway (an independent company operated by the GWR) opened a single track route to Aylesbury from Wycombe. Further competition for Aylesbury traffic arrived during September 1868, in the form of the Aylesbury and Buckingham Railway, which again was operated by the GWR. It was known that the Metropolitan Railway was looking to build a line to Aylesbury during the late 1880s, which was when the LNWR decided to take positive action by building a new Aylesbury terminus, which was located nearer to the centre of the town, and which was opened in June 1889.

However, even this new station did not protect London bound passenger traffic vanishing from the Cheddington route. The bold newcomer on the Aylesbury scene was the rapidly expanding Metropolitan Railway (MR), under the chairmanship of the flamboyant Sir Edward Watkin. The MR was keen to become a main line railway, rather than just part of the London underground network. It was soon apparent that London-bound commuters preferred the MR's fast and direct services

Track work being carried out at Aylesbury. The fact that the inscription on the picture shows "Met & GCR" indicates that the photo was taken between 1906 and 1923, when the Great Central Railway (GCR) was absorbed into the London & North Eastern Railway. (Courtesy; TLOSA).

to the centre of the capital, rather than the slow train to Cheddington, where a change had to be made for London Euston. On New Years Day 1894, the joint MR/GWR Aylesbury station was opened for public use. This was followed within a few years by the construction of a new main line into Marylebone, this being known as the Great Central Railway (GCR), which gave Aylesbury based travellers an even greater choice of services. It was soon clear that the Aylesbury-Cheddington line had had its heyday, although it still retained a modicum of both passenger and freight traffic.

The Cheddington line finished up as something of a rural backwater. It became part of the London, Midland and Scottish Railway (LMSR) at the time of the railway Grouping in 1923, and was then merged into the nationalised British Railways (BR) network in 1948. A further, more minor change took place during 1950, when its Aylesbury terminus was renamed Aylesbury High Street, in order to distinguish it from the former GCR station. However, over a period of many years, a combination of alternative rail connections and road transport, in particular bus networks, had gradually eroded its trade. The passenger service became an early victim of the closure programme, finishing in February 1953, whilst goods traffic lingered on for a further decade, before this too was discontinued in December 1963.

Today, this pioneering line is a largely forgotten route. At Aylesbury, the former High Street terminus has been lost to road developments, whilst at Cheddington the former trackbed has become part of the station carpark. However, it is possible to note the bay platform, which is still in situ, and it is easy to imagine a steam hauled branch line train waiting in this platform. Cheddington station itself remains a busy commuter outpost, served by trains between Birmingham, Milton Keynes, and London. Sleek "Pendelino" express trains rush through, contrasting somewhat with the more orthodox electric multiple units which call at the station.

The beginning of the former line between Cheddington and Aylesbury, seen from Cheddington car park, July 2000. (MJE).

As can be imagined with a railway line that was finally closed more than forty years ago, it is hard to locate many surviving relics. Whereas other closed lines within the locality have been converted into public footpaths in their entirety, the Cheddington-Aylesbury line has had this done only on a few sections. One place where it is quite easy to find a trace of the route is at the former Marston Gate station. Although the old station building has been demolished and replaced by a new dwelling, a hump in the road passing here marks where the railway line ran. A single crossing gate post survives at the entrance to a field opposite the house. Looking into this field, it is possible to imagine the course of the old line, running towards Cheddington. Apart from this, there are a number of telegraph poles, crossing gate posts, and boundary fences still in situ at various locations along the route. Other sections have become part of private houses or belong to independent organisations.

In conclusion, it is sad to note that this pioneering railway has faded away into the mists of time, known only to railway enthusiasts and historians. Probably its main contribution was to enable both Aylesbury and Cheddington to gain a toehold on the railway network, a position that both towns retain today. As for the branch itself, it lives on only within the printed word.

FIFTY MILES FROM LONDON

VERNEY JUNCTION AND THE
METROPOLITAN RAILWAY

To anyone unfamiliar with the complex history of both the Metropolitan Railway (MR) and, indeed, of the present day London Underground tube network, it seems almost impossible to believe that the long-closed section of railway line between Quainton Road and Verney Junction formed the most northerly outpost of the "Met", as that ambitious organisation broke away from its London base and forged ever-northwards, as part of the plans of its forward looking chairman, Sir Edward Watkin, whose ultimate goal was for the MR to form the cross-London part of a Manchester to Paris high speed rail link.

The line between Quainton Road and Verney Junction began its life as part of the fledgling Buckingham Railway. This project was incorporated by an Act of Parliament in 1847, part of the original plan being to link Claydon (located on what became the London and North Western Railway's (LNWR) cross-country route between Oxford, Bletchley, and Cambridge) with Aylesbury. The LNWR, who were the major railway company in the locality, being the operators of the London to Birmingham route, were hostile to this plan, and the scheme was never pushed through to fruition. However, pressure was growing to build the new railway, in particular from a group of local landowners, the most influential of which were the then Marquis of Chandos (who in due course became the third and final Duke of Buckingham and Chandos in 1861) and Sir Harry Verney, the MP for Buckingham. These two distinguished gentlemen became Chairman and Vice-Chairman of a new scheme, the Aylesbury and Buckingham Railway (ABR), this project being incorporated by an Act of Parliament in August 1860.

Station sign at Verney Junction, circa 1950s.
(Courtesy; David Lawrence/Hugh Davies Photographics).

Whilst the original line was to have been a direct link between Claydon and Aylesbury, the new route was more circuitous, linking Claydon to Quainton Road, and then to Aylesbury. It passed near to the Marquis' estates at Wootton. Once the Act of Parliament had been passed, construction was put in hand, and the new line was opened to traffic on the 23rd of September 1868. In recognition of the fact that the link between the ABR and the LNWR at Claydon was situated on Sir Harry Verney's land, the new junction created was named Verney Junction. At the start of its working life, the ABR was operated by the Great Western Railway (GWR), with locomotives and rolling stock provided by that erstwhile establishment. Prior to the opening of the ABR, the GWR had made an advance into LNWR territory with the building and opening of the route from Wycombe to Aylesbury, this line being completed in October 1863. In another of the political wranglings that marked the railway building era of the nineteenth century, the GWR was keen to take on the ABR, thus enabling Paddington's empire to plant a foot within LNWR territory.

One result of the operating agreement between the ABR and the GWR was that the Wycombe Railway, which had been constructed as part of the GWR "broad gauge" network (the gauge being 7 feet and 1/4", as opposed to the standard 4ft 8.5" adopted by other main line railways), was converted to the narrower gauge soon after the opening of the ABR, this work being completed in October 1868. It was the first part of the GWR network to be converted, a momentous task which was not completed until 1892. Staff-wise, the footplate crews were employees of the GWR, whilst all other railway workers belonged to the ABR. The smaller concern remained independent of its larger neighbour until July 1891 (although a chance for the ABR to become part of Paddington's empire in 1874 was missed), when it became part of the then rapidly expanding Metropolitan Railway. By this time, in addition to Quainton Road, three more intermediate stations had been built and opened along the Verney Junction to Aylesbury route, these being Winslow Road, Grandborough Road and Waddesdon Manor.

The Metropolitan Railway (MR) was constructed as the world's first underground railway, the intial 3.5 mile section between Farringdon Street and Bishops Road (this latter station being located at Paddington) opening for public use in January 1863, the start of today's London Underground network. Despite the views of many sceptics, the new line was an immediate success. However, the owners of the MR were looking to build something more than merely an underground railway, and began to push northwards from Baker Street, starting in the late 1860s. Progress was rapid, and Harrow-on-the Hill was reached in 1880, Rickmansworth in 1887, Chesham in 1889, and Aylesbury in 1892. The taking over of the ABR was the final step in the expansion programme of the MR. By this time, a remarkable man had become chairman of the MR, this being Sir Edward Watkin. He was a far-thinking individual, who was also chairman of both the Manchester, Sheffield and Lincolnshire Railway (later to become the Great Central Railway), and the South Eastern Railway. He had an ambitious plan to use these three railways to form the nucleus of a Manchester to Paris rail link, via a channel tunnel.

Verney Junction became the limit of the MR's main line because the Great Central Railway (GCR) was making large strides during the latter part of the 1890s with the extension of its main line from the Midlands to a new terminus at London Marylebone. The two railways eventually linked up at Quainton Road, the new route being opened for passenger traffic during March 1899. As far as Verney Junction was concerned, the new main line bypassed the link from Quainton Road, thus making it something of a railway backwater. The two companies then decided to put the whole of the line between Verney Junction and Harrow South Junction under joint control. This state of affairs lasted from April 1906 to January 1923, when the GCR became part of the London and North Eastern Railway (LNER). The idea of having an umbrella organisation, which became known as the Metropolitan and Great Central Joint Committee, was to smooth working relationships between the two companies. These had been somewhat fraught since 1899, the result of two ambitious organisations meeting "head-on".

Verney Junction therefore became the terminus of a very efficient railway line from Baker Street and Aldgate. Although electric traction had been introduced onto the underground network, with the opening of London's first deep-level tube, the City and South London in 1890, steam was still king at the beginning of the twentieth century as far as the MR was concerned. The period of time from the 1890s until the MR became part of the London Passenger Transport Board (or London Transport as it eventually became known) in 1936, was a golden period, dominated by the expansion of what became known as "Metroland", a scheme under which many acres of countryside located near to the MR's system was converted into housing, to be bought by people who worked in London, and who would use the MR to commute to their place of work. Although Verney Junction and the area north of Aylesbury was destined not to be part of this pipedream, Verney Junction was the starting point of a Pullman car service to Baker Street. Two such vehicles, "Galatea" and "Mayflower", were employed as dining cars on early morning commuter services and late night trains run for the benefit of theatre-goers. This service commenced in 1910 and ran until the 1930s, passengers being charged a moderate supplement to their normal fare for the privilege of travelling in style.

After the MR's takeover by London Transport (LT), changes were made by the new owners regarding the services being operated north of Aylesbury. One of these changes was the withdrawal of passenger services between Quainton Road and Verney Junction in July 1936, due to low levels of passenger usage, although freight traffic was to last for a further eleven years, until September 1947. This was due to the demands of the Second World War, when the line was used as an alternative route for goods trains to and from the capital, providing extra capacity during those dangerous times. However, in an effort to increase line capacity and to speed up the flow of traffic, a connecting spur was built to link the LNWR and GCR lines at Calvert, which was located where the GCR main line to Marylebone and the LNWR Oxford-Cambridge route crossed each other. Much freight traffic was diverted away from the Verney Junction route, and, once peace returned in 1945, its fate was sealed, leading to closure two years later. Over the next twenty years or so, the story of the railway system in the surrounding area was one of decline and closure. Main line services to Quainton Road ceased in March 1963, with the former GCR trunk line to London Marylebone being closed as a through route in September 1966, whilst the Oxford to Cambridge route had its passenger service withdrawn in January 1968, although freight traffic survived for a few more years.

The present day picture is somewhat brighter. The central section of the Oxford to Cambridge line, the Bletchley to Bedford route is still very much alive and kicking, currently being marketed as the "Marston Vale" line. The suburban network that begins at Marylebone, and which runs as far as Aylesbury and High Wycombe, is the responsibility of Chiltern Railways, with their fleet of smart diesel multiple unit trains, whilst the Metropolitan Line of the tube network provides an intensive service to Watford, Uxbridge, Chesham, and Amersham. The Buckinghamshire Railway Centre can be found at Quainton Road, and

The remains of the level crossing at Verney Junction, late 2007. (MJE).

is home to a wonderful collection of locomotives, rolling stock, and railway-related artifacts. On the other hand, the former route to Verney Junction is now confined to the history books and to the memories of a diminishing group of people. Traces of the old line, such as cuttings and filled in bridges, can be spotted by the eagle-eyed, whilst the station house at Verney Junction has become a private residence, and the two platforms on the Oxford-Cambridge route are still in situ, although very much overgrown. The railway tracks here can still be found, although, once again, very overgrown. Care should be taken whilst using the level crossing here.

In conclusion, what remains of Verney Junction is a sad end to what was once an efficient way of travelling to London. However, it should be realised that this rural part of Buckinghamshire was spared the mass development that took place in other parts of "Metroland", thus retaining its quiet country atmosphere.

A DUKE'S BRANCH LINE

THE QUAINTON ROAD
TO BRILL TRAMWAY

To the casual observer, the long defunct 6.5 mile branch line between Quainton Road and Brill may seem like many other similar branch lines dotted up and down the country, which have now been consigned to the pages of history. However, its origins were somewhat different to those of most other lines, as it was the brainchild of the Third Duke of Buckingham and Chandos, who wished to construct a railway route to serve his estate at Wootton.

The Duke of Buckingham had the idea of building what became a tramway style light railway in order to transport a combination of agricultural produce and minerals to and from his estates. As related in a separate chapter, the Duke had been chairman of the scheme which eventually became the Aylesbury and Buckingham Railway (ABR). This route was opened for public use in September 1868 and included a station at Quainton Road, located roughly halfway between the two ends of the line at Verney Junction and Aylesbury. The new branch was originally laid between Quainton and Wootton. As the route was to be built more or less entirely on the Duke's land, no Act of Parliament was required before construction commenced in September 1870. The Wootton section was opened for use in April 1871, and further extensions were made, firstly to a brickworks that was located near the village of Brill (this being brought into service in November of the same year), whilst the final link to the Brill terminus was ready for traffic during mid-1872. As with many railway stations, Brill was located some way from the place that it was meant to serve. In January 1872, public demand from the residents of Brill forced the introduction of a passenger service, utilising a single Aveling and Porter built steam locomotive and a borrowed carriage. However, the good people of Brill were forced to walk up and down a steep hill to and from the station!

Once the branch had been completed, there were five intermediate stations to be found along its length. From the Quainton end of the line, trains called at Waddesdon Road, Westcott (where a siding linked the branch to a nearby gasworks), Wootton, Church Siding and Wood Siding. At Church Siding, a line of 1.5 miles was constructed in order to serve a coal wharf which was situated at Moate Farm, located upon Kingswood Lane. This particular line was in use between 1871 and 1910, when the wharf was closed because of flooding, and was unusual insomuch as it used horse traction to haul the freight trains. In its early years, the Brill branch was known simply as the Wootton Tramway; however, it was later re-named the Oxford and Aylesbury Tramroad, this being to reflect an abortive scheme to build an extension as far as Oxford. Although this scheme was eventually abandoned in 1893 due to several factors, including a lack of finance, plans were also made to run through trains to London. The Duke of Buckingham had earlier passed away in March 1889, the interests in the line passing to his nephew, Mr Gore Langton, the Earl Temple. During his life, the Duke had put together a staff rule book for the line, a publication which included a list of fines for people who broke one or other of the rules drawn up. For example, smoking was forbidden whilst on duty, anyone working whilst intoxicated was liable to instant dismissal, and if a driver did not have his engine ready for service by the required time, he could be fined 1 shilling. If such a delay was caused by his assistant, the poor old driver would have to pay a portion of the fine. Hard times indeed!

Although the London through train plan joined the Oxford extension scheme in never coming to fruition, improvements were being made to the line as the nineteenth century drew to a close. The original station at Quainton Road had been constructed at right angles to that of the ABR. This was originally sited to the north of where the present day road overbridge is located. It was not until 1896 that the present day station was built, an establishment which included a bay platform built especially for the Brill train. The original line, which had been laid on longitudinal sleepers was relaid in the conventional way, whilst both stations and level crossings were upgraded, with new buildings being added to the stations to improve the lot of the branch's passengers.

The next major event in the life of the Brill line came in December 1899, when the fast expanding Metropolitan Railway took over the route's lease, this including an option to buy the line outright, an option which was never taken up. By this time, the motive power fleet on the branch was made up of a trio of Manning Wardle 0-6-0 saddle tank engines, these being named "Brill No 1", "Wootton No 2", and "Huddersfield". An eight wheeled carriage, hired from the Metropolitan, was the sole vehicle of its type used on the line. During the early years of the twentieth century, the Manning Wardles were replaced by Metropolitan tanks of various types, until a pair of veteran Beyer Peacock built 4-4-0s, numbers 23 and 41, made their home on the line, having been displaced from their original haunts in London. These locomotives spent a semi-retirement working the branch until its final closure, some thirty years later.

Events elsewhere conspired against the little line. In April 1906, the branch came under the control of the Metropolitan and Great Central Railway Joint Committee, this organisation being formed to smooth out the differences that had arisen during the period of time since the Great Central Railway (GCR) had built its main line from the Midlands to join up with the Met at Quainton Road during the 1890s. It was a Parliamentary Act of 1899 that led to the final downfall of the Brill branch. In that year, the GCR and the Great Western Railway (GWR) were allowed to begin building a joint route from Princes Risborough to Grendon Underwood, north of Quainton Road. Quite apart from providing the GCR with an alternative and faster line into London, it also featured a new station at Wootton, passing over the branch line. Passengers who had been using the Brill branch now found that there was a better alternative to the slow, antiquated service on offer. Fast trains using the GCR/GWR route could access both London and the Midlands in much quicker time.

A move was made in the 1920s to sell the line to the GWR. However, nothing came of this initiative, and the branch eventually became part of the London Passenger Transport Board (LPTB) in 1933. Two years later, LT declared that it did not wish to continue running services north of Aylesbury, and it was decided to close the Brill branch at this time. The final train ran on the 30th of November 1935, the closure even being reported by The Times newspaper. This somewhat eccentric route had passed into history after a life of some sixty four years.

Looking towards Quainton Road, upon the trackbed of the former line between there and Brill. Visitors to the Buckinghamshire Railway Centre can park their cars either in a field on the opposite side of the road seen here, or by driving up the road, over the railway footbridge, and taking a sharp right hand turn, in order to access the main entrance 27/8/07. (MJE)

It is remarkable to note that reminders of the Brill branch can be found, even to this day. Two of the steam locomotives used, Aveling and Porter 0-4-0 no 807 and Beyer Peacock 4-4-0T no 23 have survived the years, and can be found today at the superb London Transport Museum in Covent Garden. The Buckinghamshire Railway Centre (BRC) at Quainton Road utilises the former branch bay platform for the benefit of passengers using one of their two running lines, the former wooden shelter now playing host to a photographic exhibition about railways in the local area. Elsewhere within the BRC, other relics of the line are located. Beyond the boundaries of the BRC, traces of the line can still be found. Some of the former trackbed has been included in a circular walk known as the "Tramway Trail". This route begins in Quainton village, following the route as far as Westcott. From here, the walk circumnavigates the back of Waddesdon Manor, accesses the village of Waddesdon itself, and returns to Quainton, crossing the railway line to Aylesbury in the process.

For the more ambitious individual, relics of the route can be found all the way to Brill, the most notable example being the original station building at Westcott. This is situated to the left of the former station house which itself is now a private residence. This location was also the site of a level crossing. Further up the line at Wootton, a second station house can be found, once again in use as a private dwelling, whilst at Brill itself, although the station building has vanished, a third station house is still in situ. Brill Hill, which leads to the village of Brill itself, begins at this point, and it must have been many a weary passenger who made his (or her) way up this gruelling climb at the end of a hard day's work! Other traces of the old line can be found in the fields surrounding the hamlets along its former route.

The Brill branch was a line that existed for many years on a small dict of freight and passengers, in the end being superseded by more modern routes, in particular the joint GWR/GCR line which was to be found underneath the nose of the older route at Wootton. On being taken over by LT in 1933, it is hard to imagine a greater contrast between the branch and the smart new underground system being built and expanded from its original base in the centre of London, the red electric trains used being worlds away from the antiquated tank engines (the original class members pre-dating the branch itself), hauling a single, obsolete coach to a distant Buckinghamshire outpost. Such, however, is the charm of

*A view taken at Westcott, standing on another part of the redundant
Brill branch trackbed. The former station building is situated behind the
photographer, and this particular view is taken looking towards Brill 27/8/07.
(MJE)*

the country branch line, and it is good to see that the line still lives on
in the memories of local people, in the printed word, and in the form of
the various artefacts which have survived destruction and which have
remained in situ.

"NOBBY NEWPORT"

THE WOLVERTON TO
NEWPORT PAGNELL BRANCH LINE

Since the 1960s, the new city of Milton Keynes has arisen out of the Buckinghamshire countryside. Its modern shopping centre and housing estates are very "state of the art" and provide a pleasant environment, both for the people who live there and for the many visitors. It is pleasing to note that the recreational wellbeing of the city's citizens are catered for in a number of different ways, including the provision of a comprehensive network of footpaths, designed to accommodate both foot pedestrians and those on bicycles. This web of public footpaths is known as the "Redway System", and can be found in and around the city. One small part of this network is called the "Railway Walk", and takes in the majority of the now-closed branch line that ran between Wolverton and Newport Pagnell.

The origins of this line lie in the expansion plans of the fledgling London and Birmingham Railway Company (LBR), the custodians of the first main line in the world which ran between London Euston and the "Second City". The LBR wanted to build a factory, which would construct all of its locomotives and rolling stock. Wolverton (which was a small village prior to the coming of the railway) was chosen as the site for this new undertaking. The original Wolverton Works was opened as early as 1838 (the same year that the main line to Birmingham was completed), and the LBR, keen to look after its staff, also constructed houses, a church and schools within the vicinity. Soon after this, the LBR was absorbed by a company which was to become one of the major organisations of its type in Britain, the London and North Western

Railway (LNWR). In 1846, in a major change of policy, the LNWR decided to move locomotive construction to another small village further north, which soon became known the world over as Crewe, one of the most famous railway works of all time. It was then decided that Wolverton should concentrate solely on carriage building, and thus it remained one of the most important facilities on the LNWR system.

A second major company arrived in Wolverton during 1878, in the form of McCorquodale & Company. This new organisation specialised in large volume stationery and printing, including the manufacture of tickets for both railways and tramways. This company, together with the LNWR works, were the two principal employers in the locality for many years, and drew their workforce from all around the surrounding area. It was imperative that some kind of adequate transportation arrangements were in place for the benefit of these large numbers of people.

The story of the Newport Pagnell branch line began in June 1863, when an Act of Parliament was passed to agree the construction of a four mile route between there and Wolverton. Part of the line's trackbed was constructed along the route of the former Newport Pagnell canal, which had been bought out by the LNWR, prior to building work beginning. There were two intermediate stations along the line, these being located at Bradwell and Great Linford. In an unusual move, the line was opened for goods traffic prior to the passenger service, the former event taking place towards the end of 1866, whilst the latter began on the 2nd of September 1867. Business was brisk on the new route (mainly carrying the employees of the railway works, and, after 1878, those employed at McCorquodales), and the timetable was expanded to the point where there were thirty workings per day, each train timed to take twelve minutes to complete the journey. A single steam locomotive was based on the line to haul the passenger service, and these engines were soon dubbed "Nobby Newport" by the local population. A goods service was run mainly for the benefit of companies located in Newport Pagnell.

The LNWR had ambitious plans for the branch. Towards the end of the nineteenth century, a scheme was drawn up to extend the line from Newport Pagnell to Olney, where a connection would have been made

LMS 2-6-2T 41223 arriving at Bradwell station on the Wolverton to Newport Pagnell branch line, 12/5/1962. (Courtesy; B.W.L. Brooksbank/Initial Photographics).

with the Midland Railway route between Bedford and Northampton. One wonders how this junction would have operated on a day-to-day basis as the LNWR and the Midland were deadly rivals, a situation which caused considerable problems when both companies became part of the London Midland and Scottish Railway (LMSR) at the time of the railway Grouping in 1923. However, after some initial construction had been carried out, the project was suddenly curtailed. Early in the new century, in 1904, the LNWR drew up a plan to electrify the branch. It was thought that such a scheme (similar to lines elsewhere in the country), would save money on daily running costs. Once again, however, this project never came about. One plan that did see the light of day was the construction of a spur at Wolverton in 1900 which connected the branch to the up slow running line of the Euston-Birmingham route.

The idea behind this was that the LNWR Royal Train (which was based at Wolverton) could be turned on the triangle of lines that was created by the building of the spur. In later years, the triangle was also used for turning larger steam locomotives.

Throughout its life the line led an uneventful existence, becoming part of the local community and a cornerstone of the local economy. The LNWR designed tank locomotives used during the early part of the line's existence gave way to more modern engines designed by Henry Ivatt, the last Chief Mechanical Engineer of the LMSR. The passenger trains became a "push-pull" type affair in later years, and some workings were even mixed passenger and freight combinations. These were an early attempt to cut running costs and fight off road competition. However, the decline had already set in, and, despite a vigorous campaign by local people, the passenger service was withdrawn in September 1964. Goods services lingered on for a little longer, but these were wound up during 1967.

Bradwell station, looking towards Wolverton, on the branch that ran between there and Newport Pagnell. The majority of the trackbed has now been converted to a public footpath 19/8/07. (MJE)

Today, "Nobby Newport" is still part of the local transport network, although as part of the aforementioned "Railway Walk", rather than as part of the rail network. Beginning at the present day Wolverton main line station, a walk of around half an hour will suffice to join the path at the site of Bradwell station. Leaving Wolverton station, the road outside the boundary fence should be crossed, and then the footpath followed to a major road roundabout, at which an underpass connects with a second path on the far side. A right hand turn should be made at this point (following the signs for New Bradwell). A path to the left appears after a few minutes; this leads into New Bradwell, and crosses a small river before arriving within an old fashioned housing estate. A main road can be seen ahead at this point. This is Newport Road, and prospective walkers should continue along this road until a right hand turning, known as Bradwell Road, is reached. This road proceeds up a hill, over a canal and past a public house. Beyond the pub is the bridge

Great Linford station, again looking towards Wolverton. This was the second of the two intermediate stations on the Wolverton to Newport Pagnell branch 19/8/07. (MJE)

spanning the "Railway Walk", from where a flight of steps can be used to access the former trackbed.

At Bradwell Road the station platform is still in situ, although it is somewhat overgrown with vegetation. The path itself is well tarmaced throughout the whole of its length, and does not feature any sharp gradients, therefore being equally suitable for both foot pedestrians and cyclists. Although passing adjacent to both housing estates and industrial units, the walk is essentially rural in character and makes for some very pleasant exercise. As far as the railway enthusiast is concerned, the only pieces of surviving railway infrastructure are the single platforms at both Bradwell , as previously mentioned, and at the other former intermediate station at Great Linford, together with a semaphore signal post just outside the site of Newport Pagnell station. Some of the bridges used to span roads and rivers, together with a few overbridges, also survive.

A semaphore signal post, sadly minus a signal. This is located just outside what was the terminus at Newport Pagnell, and is the only evidence that a railway station was ever located there, the rest of the site having been taken over by houses and offices 19/8/07. (MJE)

Unfortunately, all traces of the station buildings at both Bradwell and Great Linford have long since vanished, and the site of Newport Pagnell has been erased by a combination of houses and offices.

In summing up, it is good to note that the line still remains a useful transport link in its new role as a public footpath. This in turn keeps alive the memory of the old route, letting new generations know that a railway did once run along this stretch of path. The spirit of "Nobby" is still very much alive and kicking!

PRESERVATION

A pair of vintage Bedford lorries seen taking part in a Buckinghamshire Railway Centre Commercial Vehicle Display in mid 2007. Both vehicles illustrate the fact that both the private railway companies and the nationalised network ran (and still run) large fleets of road vehicles. (MJE).

A METROLAND SURVIVOR

THE BUCKINGHAMSHIRE
RAILWAY CENTRE

There is no doubt that the the British railway preservation scene is in excellent health, with many different centres located all over the country, ranging from miniature railways and museums to full length lines, re-creating the past by having restored former parts of the national network. One of the senior organisations within this movement is the Buckinghamshire Railway Centre (BRC). From the early visions of a number of far seeing pioneer members in the late 1960s, the BRC has grown into a major player on the preservation scene, and is home to a number of unique railway exhibits.

The original Quainton Road station first appeared on the national network as far back as 1868. It was constructed as part of an early railway scheme known as the Aylesbury & Buckingham Railway (ABR). This line was incorporated by an Act of Parliament in August 1860, the idea being to build a line from the now-closed Verney Junction (which was located on the London & North Western Railway's cross-country route between Oxford, Bedford, and Cambridge) to Aylesbury. The new line was fortunate because it had the support of two major landowners in the area, these being the Duke of Buckingham and Sir Harry Verney (after whom Verney Junction was named), the MP for Buckingham. The Duke and Sir Harry became, respectively, chairman and vice chairman of the new railway. The ABR was opened to traffic on the 23rd of September 1868, and, as well as Quainton Road, it also boasted stations at Winslow Road and Grandborough Road. Initially, the locomotives and rolling stock were provided by the Great Western Railway (GWR);

A former Great Western Railway "Castle" class locomotive "Defiant", which now resides in the Rewley Road Visitor Centre at the BRC, seen in 2006.
(MJE)

this was because the promoters behind the ABR were looking to extend their new line into GWR territory, and, as a favour, asked the GWR to operate the original part of their line. The GWR, not wishing to miss an opportunity to extend their sphere of operations into London & North Western Railway (LNWR) territory (the two companies were deadly rivals), were happy to oblige, although the ABR was never taken over by the bigger concern. Instead, it remained an independent company until July 1891, when it was absorbed by the rapidly expanding Metropolitan Railway.

In 1871, Quainton Road became a junction, when the 6.5 mile line to Brill was opened. The Duke of Buckingham was the driving force behind this line, as it was constructed mainly for the purpose of serving his estates at Wootton. No Act of Parliament was needed to authorise construction as the route was laid almost entirely on the Duke's land. The line was completed by the middle of 1872. Local public demand was such that, in addition to those trains run for the benefit of the Duke's estate, a passenger service was initiated in January 1872.

In 1899, Quainton Road became part of a joint railway, the two companies in question being the Metropolitan and the Great Central (GCR). The catalyst behind this turn of events was the one-time, larger than life, chairman of both companies, Sir Edward Watkin. Sir Edward assumed the chairmanship of the GCR as early as 1864, when it was a mere provincial line between Manchester and Grimsby, and it was known as the Manchester, Sheffield, and Lincolnshire. Although the fledgling line expanded quickly during the latter part of the Victorian era, Sir Edward was keen to build an extension to London. A bold plan was unveiled in the early 1890s, the new main line running from Annesley, south of Nottingham, to Quainton Road, where it would then share the tracks of the Metropolitan until it reached Hampstead, whereupon it would divert into its own terminus at London Marylebone. Sir Edward had also taken the Chairmanship of a third railway company, the South Eastern, and began to harbour dreams of a Manchester to Paris service, via a Channel Tunnel. The London extension scheme was authorised by Parliament in 1893 and was completed by 1899, the last main line to be built in Britain until the Channel Tunnel Rail Link around one hundred years later. As part of this work, Quainton Road station was rebuilt into the layout familiar today, complete with a bay platform for the Brill branch train.

Despite the high hopes of Sir Edward Watkin, the GCR was not a commercial success. Much of its potential traffic had already been taken by the rival Midland Railway (MR) , whose main line to London St Pancras duplicated the GCR for much of its journey. Despite the best efforts of both the GCR and its successor, the London and North Eastern Railway (LNER), inter-regional politics, and the publication of Dr Richard Beeching's "Reshaping of British Railways" report in 1961, made it clear that there was no room for both the MR and GCR in the new network. Gradually, the services on the GCR were either withdrawn, lost to the all-conquering motor vehicle, or transferred to other routes. The result was that the GCR main line between Calvert and Sheffield was closed to all traffic in September 1966. Prior to this, Quainton Road had been closed as an economy measure in September 1963. However, whilst the GCR faded into history, for Quainton Road a new era was about to begin.

Quainton Road station as seen in 2006, looking northwards. Although the station is owned by the BRC, the tracks seen belong to Network Rail, and are mainly used by rubbish trains travelling to Calvert. (MJE).

During the 1960s, the fledgling British railway preservation movement was slowly expanding, the beginnings of the splendid organisation seen today. One of the early groups was the London Railway Preservation Society (LRPS) who had collected a number of locomotives and rolling stock, which was stored at various sites throughout the Home Counties. The members of the LRPS wanted to bring these items together at a single location, one that would enable the public to see their collection, and one that would have the potential to become a full-blown railway museum. After a long search, Quainton Road was chosen as the new centre, and the LRPS became the Quainton Railway Society.

Why Quainton Road? There were three main reasons why this semi-rural location was chosen, the first being that it was a convenient one in relation to where the QRS members lived. Secondly there was much room available, and, in a far-sighted move, the freehold to both yards was purchased at the time that the preservationists arrived. Thirdly, the QRS had ideas of purchasing the 4.5 mile section of track between Quainton Road and Aylesbury, which would make an ideal line for running their own services. They reckoned that, with the demise of the GCR, this part of the old main line would also soon be surplus to requirements, and be closed as a result. In fact, against all odds, this line has survived in service to the present day, mainly due to a regular service of rubbish trains, coming from London and travelling to landfill sites at Calvert. While this turn of events has thwarted the aims of the preservationists, it has enabled a diesel passenger service to be run between Aylesbury and Quainton on selected bank holidays, thereby bringing more visitors

A former Great Western Railway (GWR) Pannier Tank locomotive 7715 is seen passing the station belonging to the VAMES organisation during 2006. (MJE).

on site.

Today, under the banner of the Buckinghamshire Railway Centre (BRC), the site at Quainton Road has expanded to hold a vast cross section of unique exhibits, with much to interest everyone from railway enthusiasts to casual observers and families looking for an interesting and different type of day out. One of the highlights of anyone's day is the impressive Rewley Road Visitor Centre. This outstanding structure was originally located in Oxford, and was built to a similar layout as the original Crystal Palace, designed by Sir Joseph Paxton and constructed for The Great Exhibition, which was held in Hyde Park in 1851. During the late 1990s, Oxford University wished to build their new business school on the original site of the station, and, in a generous move, helped the BRC in their plans to dismantle the station and move it to Quainton, where it has been rebuilt. Today, it has become the visitor centre, and features a restaurant and souvenir shop. Examples of rolling stock can also be found here, along with a former GWR express passenger engine, "Castle" class no 5080 "Defiant". Publicity literature relating both to the BRC and to many other museums and railways can also be found within its walls.

In both yards, a running line is included, and engines from the BRC collection can be found working, hauling both passenger and goods trains, enabling visitors to take a train trip as part of their visit. On special occasions, visiting locomotives can be found. Throughout the year, as well as the regular open days, themed events are held, including the ever-popular "Thomas", together with car and commercial vehicle rallies. Engine driver courses are also held, although these have to be pre-booked, whilst miniature railway enthusiasts are also catered for by the circuit created by the Vale of Aylesbury Model Engineering Society (VAMES). A large selection of locomotives can be found working on the half mile section of track, and the quality of workmanship employed in their construction makes them as much of an attraction as their bigger cousins elsewhere on site. Various exhibitions tell the story of Quainton and of railways in general, with the aid of various items, ranging from humble posters and pictures, right up to full size locomotives, carriages (some of which are extremely old, but which have been lovingly restored, in some cases to working order) and four wheeled wagons of all types.

7715 is seen for a second time during 2006, this time on the buffer stops whilst operating the Up Yard passenger train service. (MJE).

One of the attractions of Quainton Road is the unusualness of some of the locomotives on display. One of these splendid veterans can be found in the form of the Beattie Well Tank 30585, a little 2-4-0 engine that was constructed by the London and South Western Railway in 1874. It was originally designed for hauling London commuter trains - however, as these trains became heavier, the Well Tanks were superseded by bigger engines. The BRC example was one of a trio of Well Tanks that ended up working on the Wadebridge-Padstow line in Cornwall, a line they were suited to because of its light construction and tight bends. In the early 1960s, the three Beatties were withdrawn from service, and 30585 subsequently found its way to Quainton Road. In more recent times,

30585 has been restored to full working order, as has the other Beattie that has been preserved, 30587, which lives on the Bodmin and Wenford Railway. The two old-timers have spent much time together since their respective restorations, with 30585 taking periodic holidays in Cornwall, whilst 30587 has made the return journey to Buckinghamshire.

Another veteran on site is the unique "Met No 1", an 0-4-4 tank engine that was built by the Metropolitan Railway (MR) at its Neasden Works in 1898. After a lifetime spent working passenger and freight trains for both the "Met" and London Transport, "Met No 1" moved to Quainton in the late 1960s. It is one of only two former MR steam locomotives to survive to this day, the other being Beyer Peacock built 4-4-0T no 23, which is located in the London Transport Museum in Covent Garden. Since preservation "Met No 1" has taken part in some of the "Steam on the Met" events organised by London Underground Limited, and was in fact used in the first such event, this taking place in 1989 to mark the one hundredth anniversary of the opening of the Chesham-Chalfont branch line.

None of the above would happen without the help of the many volunteers who give up their free time to assist in numerous different ways. They have helped to make the BRC an attraction well worth visiting. Contact details for the Centre are as follows;

Post; Quainton Road Station, Quainton, Nr, Aylesbury, Bucks. HP22 4BY.

Phone; 01296-655450 (recorded information) or 01296-655720 (open weekdays 09.30-16.30 only).

Email; bucksrailcentre@btopenworld.com

Website; www.bucksrailcentre.org

THE ICKNIELD LINE

THE CHINNOR AND PRINCES
RISBOROUGH RAILWAY

uthor's Note; As with the Higham Ferrers to Wellingborough line, described elsewhere within these pages, the geographical location of the CPRR lies just outside the scope of this volume, within the county of Oxfordshire. However, in order to give a more rounded view of the preservation scheme within the locality, I would like to exercise a little "poetic licence" and bring it within the covers of this book.

Every now and again, new railway preservation schemes come into existence, complementing those that are already in situ, and adding to the rich variety on offer. In spite of the fact that the preservation of complete railways is now more than fifty years old (having begun with the Talyllyn Railway in 1950), new plans and projects continue to be put together by the active minds of groups of railway enthusiasts. One of the more recent lines to be preserved is the 3.5 mile section between Chinnor and Thame Junction, located near to Princes Risborough, this section of track having been purchased by an organisation known as The Chinnor and Princes Risborough Railway Association (CPRRA). Not surprisingly, the proud owners have decided to name their new railway "The Chinnor and Princes Risborough Railway".

The track upon which the CPRRA has made its home was originally part of an eight mile route between Princes Risborough and Watlington. The story of this branch line began during the 1860s, when local landowners began to show interest in having connections made to the rapidly expanding railway network. The original line was to have been a through route from Princes Risborough, linking Watlington with

"Phoenix from the Ashes". The charming station at Chinnor which, although newly built, is an exact replica of the structure that was located there prior to 1970. A picture taken in mid 2007. (MJE).

Wallingford and Cholsey, where a connection would have been made with the Great Western Railway (GWR) main line to London. However, because of money-related problems, the Watlington-Wallingford section was never built, although the three mile line from Wallingford to Cholsey was constructed, and today has become home to a separate group of railway preservationists, collectively known as the Cholsey and Wallingford Railway. A less ambitious plan evolved to build an orthodox branch from Princes Risborough as far as Watlington. The scheme was indeed known as the Watlington and Princes Risborough Railway Company (WPRRC) , and construction was authorised by an Act of Parliament dated 26th July 1869. The Act called for the building of a line some 8 miles and 66 chains long. Construction was started straight away, and the new line was opened for traffic on 15th of August 1872. It included two intermediate stations, these being the present headquarters at Chinnor, and Aston Rowant.

The early years of the branch line were ones of great struggle, and the new organisation was soon in financial difficulties. Things got so bad that the WPRRC's directors were forced to run the line at their own expense. Clearly such a situation could not continue for any length of time. On a number of separate occasions, ownership had been offered to the GWR, but interest was slow to come from the larger organisation. However, the WPRRC directors finally got their way when, on the 1st of July 1883, the GWR took over the line. The first job that was undertaken by the new owners was the relaying of the track. Originally, the line had been built as a light railway, and the track had been laid directly onto the local chalk. The GWR relaid the line to the same high specification as their other routes. They also looked to boost traffic by opening a series of halts. In 1906, three such stations were opened at Bledlow Bridge, Kingston Crossing and Lewknor Bridge, whilst in 1925 a further halt was brought into service, this being at Wainhill Crossing.

From 1883, up until the time of the demise of the GWR in 1947, the branch led an uneventful life, with one notable exception. In 1908, a lime and cement works was opened adjacent to the line at Chinnor. As a result, there were regular freight workings of coal and gypsum traffic, specifically for these works. Such traffic boosted the passenger receipts, and enabled this part of this line not only to remain open after passenger traffic had ceased, but also to last long enough to be preserved. During the Second World War, extra passenger traffic was generated by the presence of airfields and military sites located near to Watlington. However, with the return of peace in 1945, passenger numbers continued to fall. Despite the opposition of both local groups and individuals, it was decided by the GWR's successors, British Railways (BR), that the line should be closed to passenger traffic, and this sad event took place on the 1st of July 1957. With the exception of the cement works traffic, freight workings lingered on a little longer, until January 1961, when the section beyond Chinnor to Watlington was closed completely. Cement workings continued until 1989, when BR declared that the wagons used for the freight traffic had become obsolete. The cement works owners faced a choice between investing in new wagons and unloading systems, or transferring the freight to road vehicles. The latter course was chosen, and, in December 1989, the final cement train ran on the branch. Although this was the end of the branch's life as part of the national rail network, a new beginning was just around the corner.

In August 1989, a meeting was held, from which a new railway preservation group, the Chinnor and Princes Risborough Railway Association (CPRRA) was formed, the idea being to gauge local support for a scheme to preserve the line between these two locations. People were enthusiastic and willing to become involved in the new scheme. As with any railway preservation scheme, things began in a small way, with BR allowing the CPRRA to work on the fences and vegetation bordering the line during the early part of 1990; a year later, the preservationists took over maintenance of the whole branch as far as Thame Junction, this including all trackwork. Also during this same year, 1991, the CPRRA became a registered charity, and negotiations were started with the BR Property Board to buy the line, a task completed three years later. During this period of time, the most visible sign that the railway was coming back to life was the re-construction of a new station at Chinnor, the CPRRA's headquarters.

During the initial period of time that the Princes Risborough-Chinnor section of line was still open for cement works traffic, the redundant station buildings at Chinnor had remained standing. However, during the early 1970s, the buildings were demolished and the platform ripped up. When the preservationists arrived at Chinnor some twenty years later, they were confronted by nothing more than a grassy bank. However, in another of those "miracles" that have become commonplace within railway preservation, a new replica GWR station was to rise, phoenix-like, in its place.

The CPRRA were lucky in their quest for a detailed specification on the main station building because an identical structure located at the former Watlington station was still standing at this time, and all the necessary information was taken from there. The first part of the plan was to build a platform of two coach length, a task which was completed in 1994. During the following winter, the platform length was doubled. After sufficient funds had been raised, work began on the new building in January 1998, the aim being to re-create a typical GWR branch line station. Although professional help was employed for certain jobs, a group of six CPRRA volunteers became the dedicated "core" team, working on the building during their spare time. It was a proud moment when, on 20th April 2002, the CPRRA's President, Sir William McAlpine, opened the completed building for public use.

Much had been going on elsewhere during this time. The CPRRA had been given the "green light" by the Railway Inspectorate during the summer of 1994. This meant that a public train service could now be organised. On August 20th of that memorable year, the first passenger train since the original closure in 1957 was run, this working travelling between Chinnor and Wainhill Halt. Over the following two years, the line was extended, until it reached the current limit of operations, this being at Thame Junction. Here a loop has been constructed, in order to enable the locomotives to run round their trains.

A journey along the line begins, naturally enough, at Chinnor. The splendid station building is the centre of this charming station, serving, as it does, as a booking office and souvenir shop. The platform is reached via a barrow crossing from the access road and car park, and, prior to reaching the booking office, an old carriage body doubles up as a restaurant and buffet. This interesting item of rolling stock originally worked on the Cambrian Railway, in North Wales. It had resided in the back garden of a house located near to Oxford; however, when a house extension was required, the carriage was kindly donated to the CPRRA, arriving in 1995. Prior to the construction of the station building, the carriage body had been pressed into service as a temporary ticket office and waiting room. A similar tale surrounds the arrival of a small signal box which is currently located next to the carriage body, at the end of the platform. This historic piece of railway architecture was originally located at Mouldsworth, near Chester, and was built in 1894. In 1975, it was declared surplus to requirements, and was moved to a private garden in Berkshire. In 2007, it made the short journey to Chinnor, and is now being restored to working order.

A former GWR Pannier Tank locomotive 6430 is seen at Chinnor during 2007.
(MJE).

On leaving Chinnor, the train travels under a road bridge, and passes through a cutting, surrounded on both sides by houses. Gradually leaving Chinnor behind, the train descends for a time before passing Wainhill Halt, the first such station on the line; however, the line then begins to ascend, with the engine working hard, and soon the hamlet of Bledlow is reached, where the local cricket club's pitch can be found adjacent to the line. Pictures of this pleasant location have found their way into many railway publications in recent years, the combination of cricket match and steam trains passing by in the background being one that is almost unique in the modern age. The train soon passes by the site of the original Bledlow Bridge Halt, upon which open countryside is regained. Views of the village of Horsenden can be seen to the right, and, off to the left, can be spotted a green bridge which carried the now closed branch to Thame over a local minor road. The track swings right at this point, and terminates in the previously-mentioned passing loop, alongside which are some Network Rail sidings, used for storage of railway rolling stock.

What of the future for this fast growing railway? There are two main objectives for the CPRRA at the present moment in time, the first of these being to extend their running line into Princes Risborough itself. A lease will have to be negotiated with Network Rail before work can begin on track laying. The signal box located north of the station will be refurbished at a later date, although it is not part of the initial plan to extend the line into the station itself. There are hopes that it will eventually be possible to create a railway workshop, together with maintenance facilities for both locomotives and rolling stock. This ambitious plan is matched by an even more challenging long term one at the other end of the line. This scheme aims to relay the line between Chinnor and Aston Rowant, almost halfway to the original terminus at Watlington. Apart from track relaying, signalling equipment will be brought in. Platforms and station buildings will be constructed at both Aston Rowant and at Kingston Crossing. Once these plans have been brought to fruition, the CPRRA will have a fully operational line of some seven miles in length.

In conclusion, the CPRRA has come a long way in a very short space of time. There is much to interest both the railway enthusiast, together with families and other people looking for an interesting day out. It is well worth making a trip to this corner of Oxfordshire to discover this confident newcomer to the rich tapestry of Britain's railway heritage. Contact details are as follows;

Talking Timetable; 01844-353535.

Website; www.cprra.co.uk

FOR THE ENTHUSIAST

The national Locomotive Club of Great Britain ran its first trip to New Zealand in October 2000. A 4-8-2 locomotive, J1250, is seen on the Club visit to the Glenbrook Vintage Railway. (Courtesy of Mr Brian Garvin).

THE LOCOMOTIVE CLUB OF
GREAT BRITAIN

A SHORT HISTORY

If a casual observer were to take a glance at any of the many national railway magazines, he could well be quite amazed at the amount of railway groups and clubs that are currently in existence. Many of these organisations are locally based and have but a single meeting point. Others cater for more specialist interests, such as a type of locomotive or a particular railway. Very few have as long and as proud a history as the subject of this chapter, the Locomotive Club of Great Britain (LCGB).

It was in April 1949 that the LCGB was first formed. The initial foundation came about quite by accident, and took place during what was meant to be a gathering of part of the Ian Allan Locospotters Club, an offshoot of the publishing company that started a national "craze" by printing the first books listing the numbers of all the locomotives that were to be found on the British Railways system at that time. The meeting itself was located at St Mary's Parish Hall in Aylesbury, and the catalyst for the foundation of the LCGB was the Club's present day chairman (and member number one), Mr Jack Turner. When it became clear that no-one from the Ian Allan organisation was going to turn up, he called an impromptu meeting of all the Branch Secretaries, at which the decision was taken to form the Club. It is good to report that Mr Turner today holds the position of Club Chairman, still very much involved with overseeing its fortunes in the current era.

In the early years, visits to locomotive sheds and workshops were the main activities, this being for the dual purposes of taking engine numbers and private photography. This simple format was very successful, and by

1950, there were no fewer than thirty regional groups, most consisting of an average membership of around twenty people. In those days, there were very few national railway enthusiasts organisations, the main competitors being the Stephenson Locomotive Society (SLS) and the Railway Correspondence and Travel Society (RCTS) - both of which are still active today. The practice of publishing a "members only" news letter commenced in July 1949, and this was the forerunner of the current "Bulletin" - issued ten times each year to Club members.

The 1950s brought a new look to the Club. It was decided to move on from being a purely "spotter" type organisation, and expand into areas such as railtours. The first Club railtour took place on the 6th of September 1953, and covered a series of railway routes in the Wye Valley. A single Great Western Railway railcar was employed on this tour, in contrast to the bulk of the excursions that followed, which employed steam traction. During the rest of the 1950s, there was not a great number of tours organised; this grew in the early 1960s, when an accelerated programme of line closures and the demise of steam locomotives became the catalyst for a lot more outings. In fact, by February 1967, the "South Western Suburban" (a circular tour of lines in the southern part of London) had the honour of being the Club's 100th such event.

In May 1968 came what was probably the most widely publicised tour arranged by the Club, this being a trip from London Kings Cross to Edinburgh with arguably the world's most famous steam locomotive - 4472 "Flying Scotsman" . The tour was arranged to mark the 40th Anniversary of the first non stop run between the capitals of England and Scotland, also with 4472. The whole event had huge media attention, with a programme of the tour being made by BBC Television. In August 1968 came the end of an era, with the demise of steam traction on British Railways, the Club's own "farewell" being run on the 4th of that month.

As mentioned before, the Club was moving away from being a "spotter" organisation into something more long term. The most obvious sign of this new policy was the demise of the regional groups, and the formation of the Branches, nine of which are still in existence at the time of writing. The first Branch of all was in London, whilst further such groups began in Bedford (1958) and East Anglia (1960). By 1962, six such Branches had been formed, and a further three came into being the following year. At the time of writing, it was pleasing to note that the Bedford Branch were preparing to celebrate their 50th Anniversary in 2008.

With the end of steam traction on the national railway network in 1968, the number of tours arranged by the main Club declined, although the North-West Branch reversed this trend, arranging more than 100 such outings up to 1989. Unfortunately, for various reasons, running such trips today is no longer viable. However, over the same period of time, the Club has become one of the leading players in the organising of overseas railtours. The first such tours took place during the late 1950s, with various parts of Western Europe and Scandinavia being visited. In 1965 came the first "Continental Weekend" tour, this being a steam hauled trip in northern France between Boulogne and Abbeville. The late 1960s saw the Club become pioneers in trips behind what was then the "Iron Curtain", with countries such as Poland and East Germany being visited. Such states were still using steam traction at that time.

Since those early days, the Club have become experts in running trips all over the world. During the 1970s, tours were organised to destinations such as South Africa, India and Indonesia, whilst in the 1980s China joined the "trip list". With the collapse of the Berlin Wall in 1989, parts of the former Soviet Union were covered, including destinations as far apart as Murmansk and Archangelsk. It is true to say that the overseas tours programme is the present day "jewel" in the crown of the Club, with around a dozen trips of all kinds being arranged to various places, both short and long haul, per annum.

One of the main Club objectives is to support railway preservation. During the late 1960s, the Club became involved with preservation in a practical way, by joining up with a group known as the Sittingbourne and Kemsley Light Railway (SKLR). At that time, there was a paper mill located at Sittingbourne, owned and operated by the Bowaters Company. The railway system built in connection with this mill was of 2ft 6in gauge, and had become very extensive. However, the parent company decided to close the whole system down and use road vehicles instead, this being done for cost reasons. In October 1969, a section between Sittingbourne and Kemsley was preserved, with the Club playing a prominent part in the running of the line until 1976. Today there is still a close working relationship between the two groups. The Club even owned its own locomotive which was preserved at Kemsley Down; this being a Peckett built saddle tank locomotive "Bear". In the year of the locomotive's 100th birthday, 1996, her ownership was transferred to the SKLR.

What of the LCGB today? As mentioned previously, nine Branches help to spread the word at "grass roots" level, arranging talks and lectures, outdoor visits to places of railway interest, and organising sales and publicity stands at various events such as model railway exhibitions. The Branches can act as the initial contact point for potential new members. Once a member, all the benefits of the Club are available, including the aforementioned overseas railtours. Other facilities on offer include the unique Ken Nunn photographic collection, Mr Nunn being the first Club President. Upon his death in 1965, the ownership and copyright of his photographic collection were purchased by the Club. In fact, the collection is made up of pictures by four people, these being Mr Nunn himself, his brother Cyril, Harold Hopwood and R.P.Angus-Lewis. No fewer than 12,000 negatives are listed, copies of which can be procured for a modest fee.

Other benefits that are open to Club members include the previous mentioned "Bulletin" house magazine (this is issued to members ten times per year), access to the Club library, which is located near to Kings Cross station, club sales and stock book publications, photographic competitions and annual reunions. A further benefit of membership is the ability to buy reduced subscription rates to certain railway magazines. At both Branch and Club level, there is the opportunity to do committee work, which can be a great source of satisfaction.

In 2009, the Club will celebrate its 60th Anniversary, and there are not many railway organisations that can claim such a long life. It is stable and looks forward to meeting the challenges of the new millennium. Further information can be obtained by writing to the Membership Secretary at;

4A Northbrook Road, Ilford, Essex. IG1 3BS.

The Club website can be accessed at; **http://www.lcgb.org.uk**

The LCGB organises trips all over the world. During one such trip to the USA, in October 2000, a quartet of diesels are seen passing through the Cajon Pass. (Photo courtesy of Brian Garvin).

BEDFORDSHIRE

MR 0-4-4T 58059 arriving at Bedford on the 12.15 local train from Northampton 16/9/1950. (Courtesy; R.J.Buckley/Initial Photographics).

NATIONAL RAILWAY SYSTEM

A view of the present day Sandy station, looking towards London in October 2007. The left hand side platform is built on the defunct trackbed of the Bedford to Cambridge route. (MJE).

THE MARSTON VALE LINE

THE BLETCHLEY TO
BEDFORD BRANCH LINE

Despite the rural nature of much of its route, the Bletchley to Bedford railway line remains a vital part of the local economy, providing a valuable transport link for a number of country-bound locations to two main lines, these being the Midland route from St Pancras to Sheffield, and the London Midland from Euston to the North West and Scotland. A number of attempts have been made to close the line in recent years. However, mainly due to the efforts of many supporters and the very active local Rail Users Group, the line survives, and its train service is currently run by the "London Midland" Train Operating Company (TOC).

The history of the line began as far back as 1844 when a number of local businessmen put together ideas for a railway link between Bedford and Bletchley. The scheme, which was originally known as the Bedford Railway, was opened in November 1846 and was the first railway to reach Bedford. The line then became a part of the London and Birmingham Railway, which in turn was merged into the London and North Western Railway (LNWR). The route then became a section of the cross-country line between Oxford and Cambridge. This particular link was built in stages, the Bletchley-Oxford part being opened in 1851, and the Bedford-Cambridge section in July 1862. The original terminus of the Bletchley-Bedford line at Bedford St Johns thus became a through station. Throughout its life, the 77 mile link between the University cities had an unremarkable existence. In the late 1950s, it was proposed by British Railways (BR), that it should become part of a freight link between the East Coast ports and South Wales. As part of this plan, a flyover was constructed at Bletchley to carry the route over the London Midland main line. However, the scheme never came about, although the flyover remains in situ to this day. Both the Bedford-Cambridge and Bletchley-Oxford lines were closed in the late 1960s as a result of falling receipts.

These closures left the centre part of the link between Bletchley and Bedford as the sole survivor, and this is the railway that is in use today. On the closure of the Bedford-Cambridge line, the original terminus at Bedford St Johns resumed its old function, but only until May 1984, when, in order to bring about an easier interchange for passengers between the branch and the main line at Bedford Midland, it was decided to close St Johns altogether and divert the line over an old freight-only section of track into a bay platform at Bedford Midland. At this same time, a new St Johns station was constructed and opened.

In recent years taking a trip on the line was like stepping back in time thirty or forty years, with the service being provided for a long while by "heritage" diesel multiple units (DMUs). These trains were replaced for a while by short locomotive hauled formations of carriages. However, the service today is provided by very capable two car "Sprinter" DMUs, painted in the distinctive lime green and mauve livery of the former train operating company Silverlink. Leaving Bletchley's platform six, the line swings away to the right, leaving the main line, and passing the motive power depot on the left. A reminder of the steam age can be seen at this point, with the unexpected appearance of a water tower, again to the left of the line. Fenny Stratford is the first station, and is one of a number of stations on the line that has a main building constructed in the "half-timbered gothic" style favoured by the Duke of Bedford, whose estate the line was built over. The line itself is single track at this point, although the remainder of the line as far as Bedford St Johns is double tracked. The route at Fenny Stratford was singled in conjunction with the ill-fated flyover scheme at Bletchley.

Leaving Fenny Stratford, the line carries on over one of the many level crossings located along its length. One of the charms of the line,

Heritage diesel multiple unit 121031 is in the now defunct Network South East livery of BR, whilst 121027 carries the house colours of Silverlink, the line's former train operating company (TOC). (MJE).

as far as railway enthusiasts were concerned, were the many semaphore signals and signal boxes which were to be found in situ. However, in more recent times, not only has much of the track been re-laid, but a colour light signal system has been introduced. This is a large confidence booster for the line, ensuring a long term future and enabling it to not only provide a day-to-day branch line service, but also a secondary function as a diversionary route for the main lines at either end. At this point, the line becomes double, and it passes over the A5 trunk road, before entering Bow Brickhill. This station is noteworthy for having staggered platforms, as do one or two of the other establishments along the line. At Woburn Sands, another of the "gothic" style buildings can be found, whilst Aspley Guise, the next station on the line, has rather narrow platforms which are somewhat lower in height than the trains that serve them.

By this part of the journey, the industrial part of Bletchley has been left behind, the line becoming somewhat rural in character. Ridgmont station is the central part of the line; here trains from opposite ends of the route pass each other. A further "gothic" station building can be found here. It provides a somewhat interesting contrast with the nearby warehouses that extend almost to the boundaries of the line itself. Lidlington is quickly passed, and then follows Millbrook, from where distant views of the St Pancras line can be found. The sleek High Speed Trains and "First Capital Connect" electric units provide a contrast with the somewhat slower diesel powered "Sprinters" employed on the branch line. However, all three types of train make their own individual contributions to the well-being of the network. Passengers leaving the train both here and at the next station at Stewartby are encouraged to visit the Marston Vale Millennium Country Park.

At Stewartby, the local scene is dominated by the tall chimneys that are part of the brick-making factory. Beyond the station, a number of sidings can be seen to the left of the branch; these are known as Forder Sidings. Here brick trains are loaded ready for their journeys to all parts of the country. A second brickworks was located at Kempton Hardwicke, the next station on the line. However, although this factory has now been demolished, a boarded up signalbox remains standing, as a reminder of past glories.

The landscape becomes more industrialised as Bedford gets nearer, and the Midland main line is passed under, before the branch swings to the left, the track itself reverting back to a single formation. The new Bedford St Johns station, a single platform hidden under a road bridge, is passed at this point. A second boarded up signalbox can be seen to the right of the line just prior to the station - this gives a clue as to the whereabouts of the original terminus. Leaving St Johns, the train makes its way cautiously through the freight yards at Bedford Midland, passing the DMU stabling point on the left, before drifting into the bay platform 1A at Midland station. Here passengers have but a short walk across the platforms, whichever destination they are going to.

At the present moment in time, the future of the line seems bright.

The tiny station at Bedford St Johns, just around the corner from the end of the line at Bedford Midland, June 2006. (MJE).

An hourly service is run from each end of its route between Mondays and Saturdays, the journey taking about 45 minutes each way. There are sixteen round trips per day, although there is currently no Sunday service. As part of the upgrades mentioned above, all of the stations have benefitted from things such as better lighting, re-surfaced platforms, and improved signage. The result of all this work is to create a more pleasant environment, one to encourage the would-be passenger. The line is a useful, modern, transport link. It is also a worthy successor to the countless branch lines that once ran across the length and breadth of Britain, many of which fell victim to the axeman in the 1950s and 1960s. Long may it retain its usefulness!

Website:

The Bedford to Bletchley Rail Users Association; **www.bbrua.org.uk**

"Bubblecar" DMUs 121027/031 at Bedford Midland, April 1999. (MJE).

RAILWAY WALKS

A view, taken in mid 2005, of the two bridges that span a minor roadway south of Luton leading from the B653 Luton to Wheathampstead road. The nearer structure carried the Hatfield-Luton-Dunstable branch whilst that behind carries the Midland main line between London St Pancras and the Midlands. (MJE).

THE DUNSTABLE DASHER

THE LEIGHTON BUZZARD TO DUNSTABLE BRANCH LINE

The London to Birmingham railway line, which is mentioned elsewhere within these pages, was the first main trunk route to be built anywhere in the world, and was completed in 1838. It served as the inspiration for many different schemes, both locally and nationally. Typical of the interest shown by different parties in the years following its opening was that shown by businessmen located in the then expanding town of Luton. Although Leighton Buzzard was already known as a market town by the early 1830s (it also boasted a population of some three thousand people by this time), Luton was becoming the major industrial centre within the local economy. It was with the aim of connecting Luton to the then fledgling railway system that plans for a Leighton Buzzard to Dunstable line began to take shape.

The origins of the "Dunstable Dasher" go back to 1841, when the great railway engineers George and Robert Stephenson drew up a scheme whereby Luton would be linked to Dunstable and Leighton Buzzard, which in turn would have given Luton its desired rail connection to London, the Midlands, and the North. However, when the plan was first announced, opposition grew because of the fact that the route would have crossed an area of common land located around the River Lea. Much of this area had already been lost to various construction projects, and the local people were unwilling to see this happen again. A second plan was then drawn up by the London and Birmingham Railway (LBR), the first owners of the London-Birmingham trunk route, who had originally planned to construct a loop line, linking both Dunstable and Leighton Buzzard, as it was keen to gain a slice of local industrial traffic. However, this scheme also fell through. Although Luton was eventually to be linked to the rail network in 1858, Dunstable was much more fortunate in this respect, as a new, simpler scheme was then drawn up for a line only as far as Leighton Buzzard. In June 1845, a Royal Assent was granted, and the Dunstable, London, and Birmingham Railway Act was passed. The backers of the scheme were lucky, as the Assent also made provision for a sum of £50,000, which would act as the line's capital. Such a large figure of money (for those times) enabled the company to purchase the land required, build the line, and operate the service once completed. Work began straight-away, and the double tracked, seven mile route was opened for goods traffic in May 1848, and for passenger trains the following month.

The route itself was fairly straight-forward, with the centre part of the line being straight and level. However, each end of the branch was marked by steep gradients, especially that between Dunstable and the sole intermediate station at Stanbridgeford, which was a challenging 1 in 40. The local passenger trains were able to cope with these stiff climbs quite well. However, with the freight trains it was a different story, and heavy goods engines such as the London and North Western Railway (LNWR) G2 0-8-0s and their successors, the Stanier-designed "Black Eight" 2-8-0s of the London Midland and Scottish Railway (LMSR) were employed on much of the freight workings.

As previously mentioned, Stanbridgeford had the honour of being the sole intermediate station on the line. It was constructed and brought into service during 1849, although its two platforms were not completed until 1860. The station also featured an extensive goods yard and sidings. It was an important establishment as it was meant to serve the nearby villages of Stanbridge, Totternhoe and Tilsworth. From the beginning of its life, the line was worked by the LNWR, and records show that a passenger service of seven trains each way was provided on weekdays only. No Sunday service was operated, due to a restriction laid down by a local landowner. Freight traffic was also plentiful for much of the line's life. The majority of this traffic was generated by three sources, the first of which was coal traffic, bound for Dunstable gas works. The second was chalk, which was taken from the pits located around Totternhoe, and the third was sand, which was mined around Leighton Buzzard. This last named industry grew rapidly during the Great War, and was the catalyst for the building of a narrow gauge railway system, some of which is still with us today in the form of the Leighton Buzzard Narrow Gauge Railway. An interchange between the LNWR and the narrow gauge line was provided at Grovebury Sidings, on the outskirts of Leighton Buzzard.

A view of the former platforms at Stanbridgeford, now located within a private residence 27/8/07. (MJE)

The line's terminus at Dunstable (Watling Street) became the centre of a dispute between the LNWR and the Great Northern Railway (GNR), who operated the line from there to Luton and Hatfield. In May 1858, the first section of this line between Dunstable and Luton was opened for public use, and a second terminus built at Dunstable (Church Street). The GNR then sought a direct form of access to the LNWR branch.

As permission for a level crossing at this point had been refused by Parliament, a bridge was built, linking the two branches, at a point west of Dunstable Watling Street. It was at this time that the LNWR asked the GNR to build a new station. The GNR offered a counter-proposal to rebuild the existing Church Street terminus. The LNWR agreed, providing that it had equal access rights, an idea which the GNR rejected outright. Negotiations between the two rivals to find a suitable solution continued for a further eight years, which ended with the LNWR building a new station at Dunstable North, which was opened in 1866. The GNR's Church Street later became known as Dunstable Town.

Traffic levels on the line, both pasenger and freight, were steady rather than spectacular, although special excursion trains were a common sight, including those run in connection with football matches played at Luton Town's Kenilworth Road ground. However, once the Second World War came to an end in 1945, the familiar decline of traffic, caused by the rapid rise of road transport, began to take effect. By now, the line had become part of the nationalised rail system, and, due to the fall in passenger traffic, it was decided by British Railways (BR) that this should be withdrawn, the fateful event occurring in June 1962. Freight traffic was a little luckier, with closure to through traffic not taking place until January 1966. However, even after this time, the section between Leighton Buzzard and Grovebury Sidings remained open to accommodate the declining levels of sand that still went by rail. In the end, the all-conquering internal combustion engine even took away this trade, and the final train ran in December 1969.

What of the line today? At Leighton Buzzard station itself, various developments over the years since closure have taken away all traces of the old line. Trains used to start from a bay platform located to the left of what is now the up slow line, and a brick built two road shed was provided for the benefit of the locomotives working on the branch. This latter structure was demolished at the time of closure and the site incorporated into the station car park. Between Leighton Buzzard and Stanbridgeford, much of the trackbed has been lost to modern developments, including the A505 road, which parallels most of the old railway route. Remarkably, the station house at Stanbridgeford still remains intact, and is used as a private residence. The author was very lucky to be shown around the gardens by the owner of the house, Mr Derrick Farman. Although the goods yard has become the house's back garden, the platforms are still in situ, and Mr Farman has made a start on a project to construct a replica of the booking office. If making a pilgrimage to look at the old station, **please** ask permission first.

A view at Stanbridgeford, looking along the public footpath towards Dunstable, which has utilised the trackbed of the former railway line from Leighton Buzzard 27/8/07. (MJE)

Beyond Stanbridgeford, the remainder of the trackbed to Dunstable has been converted into a cycleway and public footpath along the lines of other such paths mentioned in this book. At Dunstable North, the site of the former LNWR station has been taken over by district council offices. Local railway preservation benefitted from the final demise of the line, as three of its signalboxes were destined for a new life elsewhere. One box moved to the Leighton Buzzard Narrow Gauge Railway, whilst the other two were transferred to the line located at Whipsnade Wild Animal Park.

In researching the history of this little line, whilst it is sad to note the closure of the former route, it is refreshing to note that some artefacts are still in situ, either on the former trackbed itself or in local railway preservation. Added to this are various jottings, including many internet entries. The "Dunstable Dasher" has not been forgotten!

THE LEA VALLEY WALK

THE FORMER LUTON TO
HARPENDEN EAST ROUTE

It is quite appropriate that some of the now-closed railway lines described within the covers of this book owe their survival into the modern day and age because of the fact that they have been converted into public footpaths. This is because they were built as transport links, as part of the then-expanding railway network, and they therefore continue to act as transport links, although aimed at foot pedestrians and cyclists. Many such footpaths have been given names in order to identify them with a particular geographical area, whilst others are more ambitious, spanning a number of different regions. A walk which falls into the latter category is the fifty three mile trail known as the Lea Valley Walk. This system commences at Luton, this being the source of the River Lea, and takes a roundabout route to Bow and the River Thames. Along the way, it takes in such places as Hatfield, Hertford, Ware and Waltham Abbey. It is made up of public footpaths, towpaths and former railway trackbeds, all of which are connected by public rights of way. One such part of the walk is the section commencing near Luton Airport and concluding at the site of the now demolished Harpenden East station, a former part of the Great Northern Railway (GNR).

This railway line formed part of the GNR's cross-country link between Hatfield, Luton and Dunstable. The origins of this line lie in the attempts of the GNR to fight off the competition from the first major railway to be built within Hertfordshire, this being the trunk route starting at London Euston and running to Birmingham, and which became known as the London and Birmingham Railway (LBR). This line had been completed by 1838, and was the starting point for many other lines, one of which was the seven mile branch line between Leighton Buzzard and Dunstable, which was completed in June 1848 by the London and North Western Railway (LNWR), the successors to the LBR. At the same time, the GNR was building its own main line. The first part of this grand undertaking, from Peterborough to a temporary London terminus at Maiden Lane, was opened in August 1850. Both companies were then looking at schemes to connect their great main lines to various towns in the locality.

A number of prominent businessmen based in Luton were also pushing for a link to one or other of the two main lines. During the early part of the 19th Century, various types of industry were expanding rapidly within the town. It was realised that the new method of rail transport offered an ideal and quick opportunity to get their products to their markets. As early as 1841, a scheme was proposed by George and Robert Stephenson to link Luton with Dunstable and Leighton Buzzard. However, this plan foundered due to the fact that some locals opposed the idea that the planned route would cut through the Great Moor, an area of common land located around the River Lea. Other areas in this part of Luton had been sacrificed for development of one sort or another, and another construction project of this type did not find favour. A subsequent GNR plan, drawn up in 1846, would have connected Luton to Hatfield - but once again, it came to nothing. The problem of Luton being left without a rail link was highlighted by the 1851 Census Return. This document confirmed that Luton had become the largest town in the whole of Britain without either rail or water transport links. It had expanded to the tune of some 16,000 inhabitants, and produced goods worth some £2m each year. It was clear that a railway link was required and at the earliest opportunity.

After the earlier misfortunes, luck was turning the way of Luton. In July 1854, a Parliamentary Notice was given, authorising the building of a separate cross-country line from the Eastern Counties Railway (ECR) at Hertford to join with the GNR at Digswell, the company formed to oversee this project being known as the Hertford & Welwyn Junction

(HWJ). At the initial meeting of the new company's shareholders, they were told about the existence of a second project to build a new route from Welwyn to Luton and Dunstable. Such a project would join with the HWJ and have the benefit of linking three major railways, namely the ECR, the GNR and the LNWR. The scheme to build the new line was authorised by an Act of Parliament in June 1855, and the route was built in two sections, from Welwyn to Luton, and from Luton to Dunstable. The latter part was the first to be opened for public use, this momentous event taking place on the 3rd of May 1858, whilst the Welwyn section came into being on the 1st of September 1860, the whole undertaking being known as the Hatfield, Luton, and Dunstable Railway.

The new railway line formed a useful cross-country link. At Dunstable, a connection was made with the LNWR branch to Leighton Buzzard. It then ran into Luton at a new station known as Bute Street. In later years, prior to reaching Bute Street, the line passed the Vauxhall Motors factory, which for many years was the heart of Luton's industrial might. From there, it travelled past Luton Hoo, and on to Harpenden, before arriving at Wheathampstead. The final connection in the link was then made with the GNR's East Coast Main Line at Welwyn, which was reached by way of Ayot. The whole line was some twenty miles in length. Like many similar lines all over Britain, the branch became a cornerstone of the local economy, running both passenger and goods services, during the course of an unspectacular life lasting more than a century. However, times were changing, and more and more of its traffic was being taken away by competing road transport. The end came in stages, with passenger services being withdrawn in April 1965, whilst goods traffic lingered on a little longer, although this in its turn was terminated during October 1967.

Thankfully, as related earlier, various parts of the line can still be seen and used as public footpaths. The section covered in this chapter commences near to the present day Midland main line, just south of Luton Parkway station. A way of accessing this part of the walk can be found by starting at Luton Parkway station itself. From here, the Lea Valley Walk is found by walking to the A505 Airport Way, very near to the end of the airport runway. From this road, an upward flight of stairs can be found which connect the A505 with the Lea Valley itself. From here, the path descends across open fields, with the Midland main line to the right. As well as the passage of trains, the peace can be shattered by various aircraft taking off from the airport, as the walk at this point is directly under the flightpath! However, once the hill is descended, the airport is soon left behind, and the B653 road to Wheathampstead (a road which runs parallel with the trackbed for much of this section) can be reached via an underpass beneath the railway line. At the road, a left hand turn needs to be made, and the walk itself can be rejoined further on, via a set of gates located on the left hand side. It is worth mentioning at this point that the B653 is a busy road, and one that needs to be crossed with great care. It is also important to note that stout footwear should be worn for the walk, as parts of it can become very muddy at certain times of the year.

The Midland main line railway is now on the left hand side, with the Wheathampstead road on the right. This part of the walk travels across open fields. The line from Luton to Welwyn ran parallel with the main line at this point, and the trackbed itself is joined once the end of the field is reached. A driveway separates the field from the woods beyond. Two railway bridges span this driveway, the nearer of which served the old branch. Upon entering the wood, the footpath ascends, and the trackbed is reached, this being almost as high as its main line counterpart. It then bends away from the main line and back towards the B653, passing first through a cutting and then an embankment. A bridge spanned the Wheathampstead road; however, this was demolished just after closure. A flight of steps leads down to the road, where great care needs to be taken while crossing. To regain the footpath, it is necessary to walk back along the road in the Luton direction, before a "Lea Valley Walk" signpost (these can be found all along the route) is seen. Here, a corresponding flight of stairs needs to be ascended to regain the trackbed, whereupon a sewage plant can be found, well protected by a metal fence. This part of the walk is very overgrown, and care needs to be taken. However, once the sewage farm is passed, the site of Luton Hoo station is reached. Almost unbelievably, the station building is still in situ, and is currently in use as a private residence. Although a high fence protects the property, a look at the roof confirms its railway origins.

Luton Hoo Station, situated about midway on the Dunstable-Luton-Hatfield branch line of the Great Northern Railway, circa 1950s. (Courtesy; A.Scarsbrook/Initial Photographics).

Leaving Luton Hoo, the footpath becomes overgrown. Once again, great care needs to be taken, as the path takes a somewhat erratic course through some woods, before reaching the overbridge with the ever-present Midland main line. In total contrast, the footpath on the other side of the line crosses into open fields, and is very much on the level. To the right can be noted an almost non-stop procession of trains, of all sorts, on the Midland line, whilst to the left, our old friend the B653 is still running parallel on its way to Harpenden and Wheathampstead. The approaching houses in the distance are those bordering the eastern side of Harpenden. Little evidence of the old railway can be found at this point, apart from various concrete fence posts, although the lower half of a semaphore signal post can be found along the trackbed within the boundaries of Harpenden itself. The final part of the walk, into the former Harpenden East station, consists of a made up footpath, bordered on both sides by houses and industrial units.

The walk ends somewhat suddenly at the site of the former Harpenden East station. Sadly, no trace remains of this former establishment, which boasted two platforms, a passing loop, an impressive station building, and even a goods shed. The whole area is now split between a housing estate and industrial units. However, a small reminder is present in the form of the appropriately named Station Road, which can be accessed at this point, and which links the B653 to Harpenden town centre, this being a walk of some thirty minutes.

In summing up, this part of the Lea Valley walk serves an essential dual purpose. Firstly, it fulfils a role as a useful form of recreation for local people, either on foot or bicycle. Secondly, it acts as a reminder of a line, which, although as far as the railway network is concerned it has faded into the mists of time, has now become part of the public footpath network. However, it is fascinating to speculate on the role that it could have played in relieving the pressure on more over-crowded parts of the rail network had it remained in situ.

MIDLAND TO LONDON

THE BEDFORD TO HITCHIN RAILWAY

Within the framework of the modern railway system, the county town of Bedford is still as important as in days gone by. Bedford station functions as a change over point between the express services to the Midlands and the North, which are run by East Midlands Trains (EMT), and the commuter trains provided by First Capital Connect (FCC), which reach not only into the centre of London but also other locations such as Gatwick Airport and Brighton. Bedford is also the starting point of one of the great survivors of the local railway network, this being the line to Bletchley, via Millbrook and Woburn Sands. This route has survived a number of closure scares over the years; however, work carried out by Network Rail to upgrade the infrastructure (including the complete replacement of its antiquated signalling system) has ensured that its future is very rosy indeed. As well as being a commuter line, it has a back up function as a diversionary route, in case of problems on either the Midland line into St Pancras, or the West Coast route into Euston. In years gone by, however, Bedford was also one end of a series of now closed lines, one of which was the branch line which meandered to the Hertfordshire town of Hitchin.

The origins of the Bedford to Hitchin railway lie in the ambitious plans of the Midland Railway (MR) to build a main line route into London. The MR itself had been formed by the amalgamation of three of the earlier railway companies, these being the Birmingham & Derby Railway, the Midland Counties Railway, and the North Midland Railway. The joining together of these three organisations took place in

203

1844, and, following the take-over of further railways, the MR became the third largest railway company in Britain. At this time, without a London bound line of its own, the MR was forced to run services to the capital using the tracks of the rival London and Birmingham Railway (LBR) south of Rugby, a move which rebounded on the MR, due to the fact that their trains were delayed by those of their rival. The LBR later became the London and North Western Railway (LNWR), which in turn became a bitter rival to the MR, a situation which caused great friction when both companies became part of the London, Midland, and Scottish Railway (LMSR) at the Railway Grouping in 1923. Plans were first drawn up as early as the late 1840s for an MR main line to the capital, and the first firm scheme was put forward in 1847, when a route from Leicester to Bedford, and then on to Hitchin, was proposed. However, a downturn in the state of the British economy at that time forced the temporary abandonment of the scheme.

By 1852, the condition of the country's economy had started to improve, and the Leicester-Bedford-Hitchin scheme became one that was in great demand from a number of different parties, not least of which were various landowners within the county of Bedford. One of their number was a Mr William Whitbread, who had pressed the board of the MR to build the new railway. He made the point that if the MR did not construct the new route, he would speak with other railway companies to see if they would bring the dream of a Bedford-Hitchin link into reality. The MR became somewhat alarmed at Mr Whitbread's words, (not doubt thinking about a potential loss of traffic), and in August 1853 it obtained an Act of Parliament, enabling it to build a double track line of just over sixteen miles between the two towns. At Hitchin, a link was made with the Great Northern Railway (GNR), from where MR trains would use the former company's tracks to access the capital. At first, the GNR opposed the building of the new line, fearing for the future of its existing traffic. However, a compromise was reached between the two companies, with the MR providing good connections with the GNR at Hitchin.

The construction of the new line took almost four years to complete.

An exterior view of Bedford Midland, circa 1960s. Note the classic cars, including models made by Ford, Vauxhall, Austin and Morris. (Courtesy; B.W.L.Brooksbank/Initial Photographics).

There were a number of reasons for this, one of which was outside the control of the MR. The early to mid 1850s were the time of the Crimean War. As a result of this conflict, the cost of both labour and materials rose sharply, and, therefore, it was decided by the line's engineers, John Crossley and Charles Liddell, as well as the contractor, Thomas Brassey, to keep all earthworks to a minimum. The result of this somewhat short-sighted policy was that the completed line had to put up with a series of steep gradients. The construction of the Old Warden tunnel was slowed by a spate of accidents, whilst the building of the four intermediate stations on the line, at Cardington, Southill, Shefford and Henlow, were slowed by a shortage of bricks. Somehow, all these problems were overcome, and the railway was opened for passenger traffic on the 7th of May 1857. To begin with, a daily service of four passenger trains in each direction was run, these beginning at the LNWR station at Bedford (the MR's own station, the forerunner of the present day establishment, was not opened until 1859), whilst freight trains began to run some six months after the passenger trains started.

When the Bedford to Hitchin service first began, all MR trains terminated at Hitchin, with both passengers and freight having to change to the GNR, for onward connections to the capital. However, in February 1858, the long hoped-for agreement between the MR and GNR, for the former to run trains into Kings Cross, was signed. To begin with, four passenger trains were run in each direction, a corresponding freight service beginning some six months later. However, problems with too many trains sharing the same tracks began to occur, with the MR coming off worse. Matters came to a head in 1862, when the GNR evicted the MR from its London terminus. It was at this point that the MR resolved once and for all to build its own London bound main line, an ambitious plan, which resulted in the opening of the route into the magnificent station at St Pancras some six years later. Whilst the construction of the new line was good news for both the MR and its widening customer base, it was bad news for the Hitchin line, which was downgraded from a main line into a secondary cross-country route. As the route had been designed originally as part of a main line, very little thought had been given to secondary passenger and freight traffic. However, a shuttle passenger service between Bedford and Hitchin was provided for local travellers, whilst coal trains from the Midlands bound for the GNR yards at Luton were routed via the Hitchin line. Economies were made, however, the most drastic of which was the conversion of the double track to a single line, except for the section between Shefford and Southill, this taking place in 1911. It was the establishment of two Royal Air Force (RAF) bases at Cardington and Henlow during the 1920s that provided a welcome boost to the line's fortunes, with many special trains, both freight and passenger, being run for the benefit of the Air Force. During 1933, Henlow station was renamed Henlow Camp, due to the importance of the military traffic, and the Camp even utilised the services of an internal narrow gauge railway system. The picturesque village of Cardington had earlier become the location for two enormous hangers that were built to house airships. The first of these two buildings was constructed in 1917 during the Great War, and the original plan was to build airships for use by the Admiralty. Only one such machine was built and flown before the end of hostilities. During the 1920s, Government approval was given for the construction of two civilian airships, and a second hanger was built at Cardington. The first of these two machines, the R100, was built in Yorkshire, and flown to Cardington at the end of 1929, three months after the first test flight of the second machine, the R101, which had been constructed on site. As is well-documented elsewhere, this latter machine crashed in France, during its maiden flight to India, and, following this devastating tragedy, the Government of the day terminated the airship building programme, and the R100 was broken up. However, the two hangers remain in situ to this day, dominating the surrounding countryside.

The former airship hangers located at Cardington, seen in late 2007. (MJE).

The introduction of competing bus services during the 1920s began a slow period of decline for the railway, which ended with complete closure some forty years later. The rise in car ownership following the end of the Second World War bit further into the line's somewhat poor receipts. An attempt to reverse this trend was made in 1958, with the introduction of a trio of light-weight single diesel railcars, which were replaced by two car diesel multiple units in 1960. However, these units were transferred elsewhere, to be replaced (ironically) by steam hauled services. It would appear that British Railways (BR) had given up the line as a lost cause, hence the re-appearance of the older form of motive power. It was decided to withdraw passenger services at the end of 1961, the date of the last service train being December 30th of that year. Over the rest of the decade, the remaining freight traffic was withdrawn in stages, the last such trains being run for the benefit of the RAF camp at Henlow, and the last working taking place in 1969. A single bright spot during this depressing time was the filming of some scenes in 1964 for the British film comedy "Those Magnificent Men in their Flying Machines", the shooting taking place around Old Warden tunnel, and featuring a Scottish steam locomotive, the Highland Railway's no 103, together with a short passenger train. It can therefore be argued that the line survives not only in the printed word, but on moving film as well.

Today, more than forty years after the line's closure, traces of the former route are still reasonably easy to find. At Cardington, the former station building has now become a private residence, looking somewhat lonely, located as it is between the village and the aforementioned airship hangers. Between Cardington and Southill, the next station on the line, the trackbed passes under, and then runs parallel on an embankment, to the minor road that connects up the towns and villages that were located along the old line. Southill station itself has become a second private house, thus ensuring its survival, whilst the supports to the bridge that carried the route across the B658 road into Shefford can still be seen, seemingly indestructible despite the passage of time. Old Warden tunnel has now found a new lease of life as a nature reserve, under the watchful eye of the Beds and Hunts Wildlife Trust. Beyond Shefford, very little can be found of the line. The station at Henlow Camp has been lost to industrial development, whilst nothing remains at the Hitchin end of the route. However, in a strange twist of fate, a small section of the trackbed has been returned to life. In May 1984, the then-terminus of the line from

Bletchley, the former LNWR station at Bedford St Johns, was closed, and the branch linked to the present day terminus at Bedford Midland via the section of the old Hitchin line that crossed the River Ouse.

In summing up, the Bedford to Hitchin line was one of many routes that was built because of railway politics, and was later condemned to a slow and lingering death for the same reason. However, its sad passing leaves a gap within those communities that it served, a gap that is partially filled by the continued existence of the various artefacts outlined earlier within this chapter. Whilst these are in situ, the memory of the old railway route will live on.

CAPTAIN PEEL'S RAILWAY

THE BEDFORD TO CAMBRIDGE RAILWAY

The vast majority of the main line railways that were built during the nineteenth century were brought into existence either to satisfy local demand, or constructed as a result of railway politics. An example of this latter strategy would be if a company wished to take traffic away from a rival organisation by building a duplicate route to a particular location. In the majority of cases, the capital required for these major feats of building work were raised by groups of individuals or by private companies. Few people had the financial muscle to build a railway by themselves. One such person who did, however, was Captain William Peel VC, who was the instigator of the section of railway line which formed the initial part of the Bedford to Cambridge cross-country route, this being the part of the route between Sandy and Potton.

Captain Peel was the third son of Sir Robert Peel, the founder of the Metropolitan Police. He spent a varied career in the Royal Navy, winning the Victoria Cross for distinguished service during the Crimean War. When this war ended, Captain Peel returned to England, looking for a new challenge. He was the owner of an estate made up of some 1400 acres, which was situated between Sandy and Potton. The idea of a railway was born as part of the improvements that the Captain wished to make to his estate, and in 1852 the strip of land along which the 3.5 mile railway would run had already been purchased, thereby avoiding the need for an Act of Parliament. Construction was swift, and the new line was opened for traffic on the 23rd of June 1857, the opening ceremony being performed by Lady Peel, Captain Peel's mother. Sadly, Captain

Peel did not live to see the birth of his brainchild. In 1857, he had set sail in the frigate that he commanded, "Shannon", for China. However, when the ship docked at Singapore, it was diverted to Calcutta to deal with a mutiny. In April 1858, during the time that he was stationed in India, he contracted smallpox during a local epidemic and passed away. One of the two locomotives that had been procured for service on the new railway was named "Shannon" after the late Captain's frigate. This engine, an 0-4-0 well-tank, has survived to the present day, and can be found at the Didcot Railway Centre in Oxfordshire.

The line was originally intended for goods traffic only, with local farm produce making up many of the trains run. In November 1857, a passenger service was initiated, utilising rolling stock provided by the Great Northern Railway (GNR). During these early years, goods traffic made up the bulk of the line's receipts, with passenger figures running a poor second. The main reason for this was that plans for an extension to Cambridge never came to fruition. Events were soon to overtake Captain Peel's railway, when, in 1862, it was purchased by one of the miscellany of early private railway companies, the Bedford and Cambridge (BCR). The BCR had begun life two years earlier as a cross-country route which looked to connect the two county towns. To save money, it utilised the trackbed of the Sandy to Potton section, even using "Shannon" to haul contractors' trains over its former stamping ground. The complete through line was opened to passenger traffic on the 7th of July 1862, with goods traffic commencing the following month. Services were worked by the London and North Western Railway (LNWR) from 1862 until 1865, when the BCR was absorbed by its larger rival. In time, the Cambridge route became one section of the 77 mile long cross-country route from there to the other great university city of Oxford.

Originally, the whole of the Bedford to Cambridge line began life as a single track route. However, the growth of traffic in the years after opening led to the Sandy to Cambridge section being doubled, although the Sandy to Bedford part of the route remained single, with passing loops; this situation was brought about by the expense that would have been incurred by having to rebuild a series of bridges that spanned rivers

A former Lancashire & Yorkshire 2-4-2T locomotive 50646, seen well away from its old haunts, at Bedford Shed 1/3/1958. The other locomotive is an unidentified Stanier 8F 2-8-0 freight engine.
(Courtesy; R.J.Buckley/Initial Photographics).

at various points along the line. When the original line was opened, apart from the station at Sandy, which provided a connection with the GNR, a new station was built at Potton, together with a halt at Blunham. Later, during the life of the line, further establishments were constructed at Willington (this being opened in May 1903) and at Girtford Halt, a latecomer to the local railway scene, this latter station being brought into service during January 1938. Traffic receipts at Girtford were very poor, and the halt was closed a mere two years later, in November 1940. On the section from Sandy to Cambridge, a further four stations were constructed, these being at Gamlingay, Old North Road, Toft and Kingston, and Lord's Bridge. To begin with, the LNWR ran eight trains in both directions between Bedford and Cambridge, with but a single service on Sundays.

The station at Sandy, roughly a third of the way along the 26 mile route, was shared by the two railway companies concerned, the GNR and the LNWR. After crossing the GNR main line on its way from Bedford, the LNWR line ran into Sandy station via a curve and a gradient. The two sets of tracks ran alongside each other for a distance of one mile. However, there was never any physical connection between the two routes, although the two rival companies enjoyed a good relationship in their running of Sandy station itself, with passenger and goods traffic being the beneficiaries of this useful partnership. However, the presence of an island platform meant that the GNR main line was reduced to two tracks at this point, thus creating an annoying bottleneck, one that would not be removed until the closure of the LNWR branch many years later.

The Bedford to Cambridge line had an unspectacular existence for much of its life. However, in both world wars, there were many special trains run for the benefit of the fighting forces. During World War Two, a petrol supply depot was constructed by the Royal Air Force (RAF) near Sandy, and a vast number of tanker trains were seen on the route, making their way mainly to the airfields located in Eastern England. This effort reached a peak at the time of D-Day in June 1944.

Post-war, as with many lines up and down the country, the rise in private car ownership, and the provision of alternative forms of transport, meant that both passenger and freight receipts began to suffer. In May 1959, tentative closure proposals were announced by British Railways (BR), but the strength of opposition from local people meant that these plans were shelved, and new diesel multiple unit (DMU) trains were introduced. Prior to this, in 1958, a scheme of a different nature was drawn up by the railway powers-that-be. This was to have involved the upgrading of the complete Oxford-Cambridge line to the status of a major cross-country route. Sadly, this bold plan came to nothing, with the exception of the flyover constructed at the south end of Bletchley station, which remains in situ to this day. A second attempt at closure was made in 1963, and once again local pressure saved the day. However, BR put forward a counter-argument, stating that the line was losing some £100,000 annually, a large sum of money for those days. The end eventually came on New Years Day 1968, which was anything but happy for the Bedford to Cambridge route, as it was closed to all traffic, except for a short section of line running between Bedford and Goldington, where a service of coal-carrying goods trains ran until the 1980s for the benefit of a power station located at the latter hamlet. The sole survivor of the complete Oxford to Cambridge route is that section running between Bedford and Bletchley, which is described elsewhere within this volume, under the guise of the "Marston Vale" line.

As a last throw of the dice, two preservation schemes were planned at the time of closure, one of these being an abortive attempt to take over the whole Bedford to Cambridge line. A more realistic plan then came about to preserve the 5.25 mile piece of track between Potton and Gamlingay. Money problems derailed this scheme, coupled with the need to rebuild a bridge crossing the line near Potton. On the removal of the remaining track in July 1969, the scheme was wound up.

Sandy station, looking towards London. The platform on the left hand side has been constructed over what was the trackbed of the former London and North Western Railway cross-country route between Bedford and Cambridge 6/10/07. (MJE)

As this book is not concerned with railways within the county of Cambridgeshire, the description that follows refers only to the section between Sandy and Bedford, although it is necessary to note that the former station buildings at Potton have now become a private residence. Sandy station has now rid itself of the former island platform, and plays host to an intensive service of commuter trains between London Kings Cross and Peterborough, together with the impressive sight of express trains running from the capital to the north-east and Scotland. Since the closure of the Cambridge line, the up platform has been re-aligned, and is located on the trackbed of the old branch. It is interesting to note that Captain Peel, the instigator behind the original Sandy to Potton part of the former route, has a memorial in the local parish church, whilst in the main high street, a public house bears his name. It is good to see that much of the trackbed going towards Bedford has been converted into a

The former section of line between Sandy and Bedford has had the majority of its trackbed converted into a public footpath. This is a view taken at Willington, which was one of the three intermediate stations on this part of the old route, looking towards Sandy 6/10/07. (MJE)

cycle and public footpath, whilst on the minor road that leads from the A603 into Blunham village, the supports to a bridge that crossed this road can still be easily seen.

In conclusion, the failure of the 1958 plan to upgrade the whole of the Oxford to Cambridge route can be seen in hindsight to be a missed opportunity to create a line that would have relieved the pressure on busier railway routes nearer to the capital. The opportunity will not come again, even in these enlightened days when railway travel has come back into political and public favour, mainly due to environmental concerns. However, its present day role as a public footpath provides a reminder to many people that a railway did once run along this stretch of Bedfordshire countryside, thus preventing it from completely fading into the mists of time.

NORTH FROM BEDFORD

THE BEDFORD TO
NORTHAMPTON RAILWAY

A s described elsewhere, the county town of Bedford is still an important one as far as the modern day railway is concerned, being well served by both express and local passenger services, and also marking the start of the "Marston Vale" line to Bletchley. Prior to the mass closure programmes of the post-war era, a further trio of lines began within the locality. Those railways to Hitchin and Cambridge are described elsewhere within the pages of this book. The third line within this scenario was the 21 mile route which meandered across northern Bedfordshire, crossed the border into Buckinghamshire, and terminated at the county town of Northampton.

As with many of the early railways, the original plan for this line was part of a much more ambitious route. This scheme was drawn up as early as 1845, by an organisation known as the Northampton, Bedford, and Cambridge Railway (NBCR). It was envisaged that this stillborn project would be a secondary line, accessing Bedford via a station located at the present day Bedford St Johns, which is today very much alive and kicking, being found on the aforementioned Marston Vale line. Financial problems prevented this scheme getting any further than the drawing board. A second plan, this time for a line linking Bedford, Northampton and Leamington, was put together in the late 1850s; however, this scheme went the way of its predecessor. In August 1864, a meeting was held at a public house in Olney by a group of local landowners and other interested parties to discuss the possibilities of a line linking just the county towns of Bedford and Northampton. A survey of a possible route was duly carried out; only one objection to the plan was received, this being from the Marquis of Northampton. The Marquis owned an area of land at Yardley and did not wish the new railway to cross this area. Far from being a problem, this benefitted the backers of the railway, as the new route drawn up ran much closer to the town of Olney, one of the principal centres of population on the route.

In July 1865, an Act of Parliament was passed, enabling construction of the new line to begin. However, many problems were encountered, and it was to be a further seven years before the new route could begin its working life. Financial problems and difficulties in finding a suitable contractor contributed to the delay. The unfortunate death in 1867 of one of the line's backers and champions, Mr William Whitbread, led to a slowing of work between then and 1870. Even inclement weather interrupted the building work; it was announced in early 1872 that heavy rain had caused damage to some of the embankments and cuttings encountered along the route. On the positive side, it had been decided before building work began that the Midland Railway (MR) would work the line. A fine new terminus was constructed at St Johns Street, in Northampton, in order to accommodate both the new route and the MR's existing services from Kettering and Wellingborough.

After all the trials and tribulations, the new line was finally opened for public service on the 10th of June 1872. Only three intermediate stations were to be found along the course of the route, these being at Turvey, Olney and Piddington. At the Bedford end, the branch was accessed from the main line at Oakley Junction, some 1.5 miles north of Bedford station itself. Despite all the problems encountered with the line's construction, it has been recorded that the new station at Northampton had still not been completed by the time that trains started running! In the beginning, a weekday service of five passenger trains in each direction was run, although there was no Sunday service. The most intensive service was in place by 1938, when the five round trips of the early years had been increased to seven. Day to day working on the line was hindered by a series of gradients located along the route. As with many stations found up and down the country, the intermediate stations at Turvey and Piddington were built some distance from the hamlets they were meant to serve. The latter was the worse in this respect, with the railway being situated some 2.5 miles from the village, a factor which did not help when the line had to battle against bus competition in later years.

In 1923, at the time of the railway Grouping, the MR became part of the London, Midland, and Scottish Railway (LMSR). For some years, things continued as before. However, in 1939, the LMSR decided to close Northampton St Johns station, and divert the services into nearby Northampton Castle. The start of the Second World War later in the same year led to an improvement in the line's finances, when an Army camp was opened near to Piddington. Many extra trains, both passenger and freight, were run to accommodate the needs of this base. As part of the general war effort, one of the running lines between Turvey and Olney was closed, for storage of war materials in this suitably rural location. However, once peace returned in 1945, the line faced a new struggle for revenue. Other than occasional special trains run for spectators bound for Towcester Racecourse, revenue was very poor.

After nationalisation in 1948, the newly formed British Railways (BR) made attempts to boost passenger numbers on the line, the most obvious sign of this being the introduction, in 1958, of diesel multiple unit trains, to replace the steam-hauled formations. However, diesel traction was still very much in its infancy at this time, and the newcomers became prone to many failures. This situation became so serious that the old steamers were brought back into service! These changes did very little to improve the line's fortunes, as the invasion of the internal combustion engine, in the form of both bus and car, had already taken away much of the traffic. After some ninety years of steady service, the last passenger train ran on the 3rd of March 1962, and yet another railway line had passed into history, save for the piece of track between Northampton and Piddington, which was retained for the benefit of the Army camp at the latter location. In February 1968, responsibility for the well-being of the line was transferred from BR to the Ministry of Defence. In this form, the route was in use up until 1986, when it too (apart from a small section between Northampton and Brackmills) was finally closed.

Despite the fact that the bulk of the line was closed more than forty years ago, traces of the route can still be found, the most obvious of which are the station buildings at both Piddington and Turvey. The former has become a private residence, whilst Turvey has been utilised as office space, and is maintained in excellent external condition, although numerous small buildings have sprung up around it, covering parts of the former trackbed. At Olney, it is still possible to see the embankment that carried the line across the A509 road from the nearby village of Warrington, although some of this has been cleared as part of a new office development. Much of the trackbed over the whole course of the line can still be accessed, and, near to Bedford, this has taken the form of the "Stevington Country Walk", along the lines of other designated public footpaths utilising old railway lines.

An exterior view of the former station building at Turvey, north-west of Bedford, on the now-closed railway route between Bedford and Northampton. The building is maintained in excellent condition by its new owners, having been converted for use as offices 6/10/07. (MJE)

In conclusion, the Bedford to Northampton route was a line built to appease railway politics rather than to meet a major transport need, despite the hopes of its early backers. From looking at old railway maps, it can be seen that Northampton was already well served by lines belonging to the London and North Western Railway (LNWR). The MR and LNWR were bitter rivals, and it could have been that the MR was trying to grab some of its competitor's trade by building the route. Revenue was never great, and its demise was perhaps not too much of a surprise. However, its transformation into a public footpath ensures that a flickering memory of the old line lives on.

PRESERVATION

An April 2006 picture taken at Whipsnade Central station with 0-6-2T "Superior" getting ready to leave on a journey around the Zoo. (MJE).

HIDDEN TREASURE

THE LEIGHTON BUZZARD
NARROW GAUGE RAILWAY

The present day railway preservation scene in Britain is a very healthy one, with a fine miscellany of running lines and museums to delight both the enthusiast and the tourist looking for an interesting day out. Narrow gauge railway preservation is very well represented, amongst which the North Wales based Talyllyn and Festiniog Railways are possibly the most famous. However, within the area covered by this book, the Leighton Buzzard Narrow Gauge Railway flies the flag for those lines of less than standard gauge, and has a unique charm all of its own.

Whilst the Welsh railways mentioned above had their origins within the local slate industry, the Leighton Buzzard Narrow Gauge Railway (LBNGR) came about as a method of transporting the vast quantities of sand that have been mined over many years within the local area. In the latter years of the nineteenth century, there were two companies that were largely responsible for the expansion of the sand industry in the area, the first of these being Joseph Arnold and Sons Limited. Joseph Arnold opened his first pit as early as 1860, this being located at Stone Lane, Heath. A second quarry was opened a little further away at Flitwick in 1902, and by 1911 the company operated eight quarries, six of which were located in the Leighton Buzzard area. Also in 1911, Mr Arnold passed away, although control of the business had passed to his sons Ernest and Albert two years earlier. The second of these two companies was that known as George Garside (Sand) Limited. Mr Garside himself entered the industry in 1885, when his first quarry at

225

Billington Road was opened. As the mining of local sand became more profitable, he opened a number of other quarries in and around Leighton Buzzard, two of these being located at Grovebury and Rackley Hill.

Orenstein & Koppel built 0-6-0T no 740 waits to run round its train at Pages Park 10/6/07. (MJE).

One problem that faced all the mine owners was how to get their produce to local railheads and canals for transportation onto the various markets. The nearest main line railway to the sand quarries was the LNWR branch line between Leighton Buzzard and Dunstable. The heavy vehicles used for transporting the sand (including traction engines and steam lorries) caused great damage to the local road system, and, as such, the quarry owners were liable to pay compensation costs. Prior to the start of World War One in 1914, the profits to be made from mining local sand were not great; this being due to the much cheaper sand that could be imported from Belgium. However, the start of that unhappy conflict, initiated by the German invasion of its neutral European neighbour, changed the whole sand industry picture overnight.

The German invasion of Belgium in 1914 cut off the supply of cheap sand to Britain. At the same time, the rapidly expanding munitions industry was hungry for vast quantities of sand, and the Government of the day had no alternative but to turn to the home based industry. Suddenly sand quarrying in Leighton Buzzard became a very profitable industry indeed! However, there still remained the problem of transporting the sand to the various transport distribution points. During the Great War, the Government paid all the compensation costs, which left the quarry owners free to concentrate on the job in hand. Once peace returned in 1918, however, this system ceased, and the quarry companies were informed that the road vehicles used during the conflict had to be sold by the end of January 1919, otherwise they would again become responsible for paying compensation costs. It was at this time that the quarry owners decided to construct a light railway to reduce costs and improve the transportation side of the business.

The Leighton Buzzard Light Railway (LBLR) (as the new system was to be known) came about as the result of various surveys undertaken during the early part of 1919, the main driving force behind the scheme being Messrs Arnold and Son. A separate private company was formed in July of that year to bring the new line into being. The 2ft gauge system was opened on the 1st of December 1919, the running lines totalling some 4.5 miles. A rail-to-rail connection was made with the Leighton Buzzard to Dunstable branch line, sand being loaded from the narrow gauge wagons into their standard gauge cousins. The nucleus of the new line now forms the present day LBNGR. There were also various connections to many of the local sand pits. The network also served two separate companies, these being the Marley Tile Works and the Leighton Buzzard Concrete Company, both of which were located to the north of Pages Park, and both of which have now closed. The terminus of the line was at a series of quarries situated near to the A5 trunk road, the ownership of which was split between Arnold and Garside, this area being known as Double Arches.

Although the line started its life by using steam traction, very quickly the locomotive fleet became made up of "Simplex" type petrol locomotives, these being much more cost-effective than the two steam

227

engines originally used. These unusual looking machines were similar to those built by a Bedford based organisation, the Motor Rail Company. They had been designed to be used on 60cm gauge railways used to transport munitions and supplies to the Allied front lines during the Great War. Both war surplus engines and newly built locomotives of both 20 and 40 horsepower engine size found their way to the LBLR over a period of many years, and some of them have survived into preservation. Fittingly, examples can still be seen on today's LBNGR. An early claim to fame for the original railway was that it was thought that the line was the first permanent system to be worked entirely by internal combustion engines - many years before the national network followed suit!

From the opening of the line until the early 1960s, a huge amount of sand traffic was handled by the LBLR. A typical number of wagons despatched on a daily basis from the various quarries at this time would be around 300 for Arnolds and half that amount for Garside. Put another way, this traffic equated to around 60,000 tons of sand per annum. However, as with many other goods that had been conveyed up to that time by rail, the sand traffic dropped dramatically over the course of the 1960s, losing out to road transport. Matters were not helped by a rail strike on the national system during June 1955. This lasted for seventeen days. During this time, much of the sand was delivered to their customers by road. Following the end of the strike, sand customers decided to send their own lorries direct to the quarries, thus even cutting out the need for any rail transport, standard or narrow gauge. By 1969, traffic had fallen to such an extent that a single daily train run from Double Arches to Billington Road was sufficient to meet quarry needs at that time. As the sand plants at Billington Road became older and less economic to run, a new washing plant was constructed at Double Arches in 1963. This spelt the end for Billington Road's now somewhat cramped plant. When, in 1969, British Railways announced the closure of the remaining part of the Leighton Buzzard to Dunstable branch line (the only surviving part being those sections of track as far as Billington Road and Grovebury), the sand trains only used the part of the line between Vandyke Road and Double Arches. It looked very much as though the LBLR was being consigned to history, following this potentially catastrophic series of events. However, something new was on the horizon.

No 740 backing onto its train at Pages Park, the headquarters of the LBNGR 10/6/07. (MJE).

During January 1967, a group of local based enthusiasts decided that they would like to build a narrow gauge railway, to be based in Watford. They decided to visit the LBLR at this time in order to purchase various items for use on the proposed line. Two of their number, Mr Brooks and Mr Harris, had a meeting with Arnolds, the result of which was an agreement between the two parties to run trains at weekends only over the full length of the line. During the following March, more progress was made when an agreement was reached with Garside to use some sheds at Billington Road for storage purposes. The new era was beginning. In those pioneering days, it was planned to operate the route along American lines, and hence the somewhat unorthodox name of the "Iron Horse Preservation Society" was adopted as a collective name for the railway's new supporters. During the rest of 1967, working parties carried out restoration duties at Leighton Buzzard, and in October that year the supporters arranged themselves into a proper society, with a committee and subscription fees.

March 3rd 1968 was a momentous day, both in the history of the LBLR, and of its newly formed preservation society. On this day, two trains were run along the whole route from Pages Park to Double Arches, these being the first run by the preservationists, the trains being made up of open wagons. Events moved quickly after this, for on the 29th of June 1968 the first regular passenger train service was started, timed to coincide with a local carnival. Steam power made a return to the line in the form of the 1877 built "Chaloner". This unique engine featured a vertical boiler (rather than the more orthodox type), and is to be found on the railway to this day. At the end of the 1968 operating season, it was estimated that there had been about 7000 passenger journeys made.

Since then, the railway has been on a steadily improving path, each year building upon the success of the previous one. At the Society's second AGM, held in September 1969, it was decided to drop the American image, and the group's name was changed to the now familiar "Leighton Buzzard Narrow Gauge Railway Society Limited". An important step forward was taken during 1970, when a lease was taken out on former stables located at Stonehenge. Over the next two years, these buildings were converted into fully equipped workshops, complete with a locomotive shed, and even a small turntable, enabling a number of engines to be kept under cover. In the early operating days, trains initially ran as far as Stanbridge Road, then the running line was re-opened as far as Leedon, and then to Vandyke Junction. Occasional enthusiasts specials ran all the way to Double Arches. However, the bright future of the LBNGR was threatened for a while in 1972, when a plot of land south of the Clipstone Brook, just outside of Leighton Buzzard, was sold for housing development. However, the local District Council decided to buy the land between Billington Road and Vandyke Road in order to help secure the future well being of the line. As part of this, a new bridge was constructed to take the railway over the Clipstone Brook.

The condition of the track itself was a source of concern during the early life of the LBNGR. Although trains had run the full length of the line from the start of preservation, the track had become worse as a result, and, in 1977, it was decided to suspend all passenger services between Vandyke Road and Stonehenge. It was not until 1983 that trains once again ran through to Stonehenge, although during the "break" much maintenance work was still carried out in the workshops there.

A typical journey along today's LBNGR would begin at the much expanded Pages Park station. Readers may wonder why your writer chose the title of "Hidden Treasure" for this chapter. It is because the narrow drive to the main building here is sandwiched between Pages Park itself and a new housing estate which has been built on the site of a former sand quarry, Pratts Pit. People unfamiliar with the area, looking for the railway for the first time, could easily miss it, and this would be a great shame, as the LBNGR is indeed "hidden treasure". There are two buildings to be found at this point, the first of these being the main booking hall, which also features a souvenir shop, from which all kinds of items relating to the railway can be procured. For those looking for something more edible, the "Dobbers Buffet" is located to the right of the booking hall, the word "Dobber" being a nickname given to the men who dug sand out of the original quarries.

Moving through the booking hall, the first glimpse of the railway itself is then seen. There are two platforms at Pages Park, partially covered by overhanging trees. The engine and carriage sheds are located at the end of the right hand platform, and this is open to visitors at appropriate times. Here the engines are prepared for their journeys; in the case of the locomotives not required, they are put on static display.

Leaving Pages Park, the park itself borders the railway on the left hand side, whilst to the right, the aforementioned housing development on the site of Pratts Pit can be seen. Indeed, much of the early part of the journey, as far as Leedon Loop, finds the railway bordered on both sides, mainly by houses, but also by industrial units. Between Stanbridge Road and Leedon Loop, two of the main customers of the original railway were located - these being the Leighton Buzzard Concrete Company and the Marley Tileworks. At this point, the train drops down the 1 in 25 Marley's Bank, this gradient being one of the steepest of its type on any railway in the country. On the return journey, it is easy to hear how hard the engines have to work when ascending this gradient.

Beyond Leedon Loop, the train passes the well known Clay Pipe public house to the left. Leighton Buzzard is gradually being left behind at this point, as more open countryside is reached. A steady climb of 1 in 45 is encountered before one of the series of unguarded level crossings located along the line is reached. This enables the train to cross Vandyke Road, whereupon it swings to the right via a sharp bend. If the visitor is sitting far enough back in the train, a good view can be seen of the locomotive at this point, before the line straightens up once again. A school can be seen to the right, and for the remainder of the journey to Stonehenge Works, the railway runs alongside Vandyke Road. This is the most rural part of the journey, and is also the highest point of the line. On a clear day, the famous "Whipsnade Lion" can be seen on an

740 at the Stonehenge Works terminus of the Leighton Buzzard Narrow Gauge Railway (LBNGR) 10/6/07. (MJE).

escarpment, located away to the right.

Stonehenge, the current terminus of the line, is reached after a twenty five minute journey from Pages Park. Whilst for many people the locomotive sheds and workshops are the main attraction, there are other things to see as well. On the single platform itself, there is a small food and souvenir shop, whilst a passing loop enables the engine to run round its train. In the case of the steam locomotives, visitors can watch them being coaled and watered. Behind the souvenir shop, a series of separate exhibitions can be found, depicting things such as a potted history of both the railway and of the sand quarries. An unusual activity which usually happens about once per month in the area behind the workshops is the "Industrial Train Display". The object of this display is to show visitors how narrow gauge railways were used in the past to serve industry, including sand and munitions. One advantage of this is that locomotives and rolling stock not utilised on the passenger services can be used, and the wagons are generally loaded using a vintage Ruston Bucyrus face shovel - another veteran of the local sand industry. A commentary tells visitors what is happening, together with other relevant information. These unusual displays have been highly successful, and have even won local and national awards.

The railway has built up a fine collection of locomotives, which is the largest of its type on any British narrow gauge line. At the time of writing, there were eleven steam engines, and no less than forty three internal combustion vehicles. The rolling stock is equally varied. In the case of the carriages, as the original line did not possess any coach stock, everything used today has had to be constructed, or procured from other narrow gauge systems, including some military ones. The wagon fleet contains many examples of types used on the LBLR, and, as mentioned above, are used on special occasions.

For the present and future, the railway is in good shape. Special events are organised in addition to the regular train service, including a "steam up week" during September of each year, followed in October by the unusual "Steam Glow", this being made up of night time train trips and photographic sessions . As well as the domestic fleet, visiting engines of both types can be found on the railway, adding an extra attraction, and taking turns on the regular services. For the future, plans are in hand to develop both Pages Park and Stonehenge, thus enabling people to get more from their visit. In conclusion, the LBNGR is a most fascinating day out, with much to interest families, casual visitors, and railway enthusiasts. Long may it continue!

Contact details for the Leighton Buzzard Narrow Gauge Railway are as follows;

Post; Pages Park Station, Billington Road, Leighton Buzzard, Bedfordshire. LU7 4TN.

Phone; 01525-373888 (24 hour information line).

Fax; 01525-377814.

E-mail; info@buzzrail.co.uk

Website; www.buzzrail.co.uk

THE "WILD" RAILWAY

THE WHIPSNADE WILD
ANIMAL PARK RAILWAY

The local railway lines that I have written about within the covers of this book have fallen into one of two categories. Whilst all the routes concerned were originally constructed to serve the needs of their respective local communities, some have remained open to the present day, whilst others have fallen victim to road transport competition and have faded into the mists of time. The line that forms the subject of this article, the railway located within Whipsnade Wild Animal Park, is somewhat unusual in this respect, as it was built for tourism and is one of the main components of this major Bedfordshire attraction.

In May 1931 the original Whipsnade Zoo was opened to the public, and was a different type of zoo to the original London Zoo, which had been opened as long ago as 1827. Both zoos were (and are) run by the Zoological Society of London (ZSL). The idea behind Whipsnade was that the animals should live in open surroundings, rather than in cages. Such a policy would enable visitors to see them in a more natural environment. The idea was an immediate success and, with the addition of good public transport, the new zoo proved popular with the general public. By the 1960s, although Whipsnade was still attracting healthy numbers of people, the opening of new safari parks elsewhere in the country provided the Zoo with some fresh competition. The arrival of a herd of white rhinoceros from South Africa in 1970 indicated that the Zoo authorities needed the public to see their new attraction in a safe way. It was felt that the building of a railway would be a good way of doing this.

Various ideas had been put forward for railways within the zoo since the 1950s. As Whipsnade Park was a privately owned piece of land, no Act of Parliament or Light Railway Order was needed to be drawn up prior to construction work beginning. Such a situation meant that the birth of the Whipsnade Railway (WR) was easier than otherwise might have been the case. In 1969 a complete narrow gauge line became available for sale with the closure of the Bowater Group Railway, which was located at Sittingbourne in Kent. This 2ft 6in gauge system had served the papermills situated there since the early part of the 20th century, but had been superseded by road transport. Not all was lost at Sittingbourne, however, as part of the line was leased to the Locomotive Club of Great Britain (LCGB) for heritage type operations. This line is still working today and is known as the Sittingbourne and Kemsley Railway. One of the original line's steam engines found its way to the Welshpool and Llanfair Railway, in North Wales, whilst no fewer than four steamers, plus some bogie wagons, made their way to Bedfordshire to form the nucleus of the WR.

Following a series of meetings between the ZSL and a group of railway enthusiasts in early 1970, the go-ahead was given for the WR to be born. To begin with, the line would be operated on behalf of the Zoo by a private company known as Pleasurerail. This organisation had been formed for the purpose of building tourist type railways in suitable locations. The WR was the first line to be built in this way; two other lines were built shortly afterwards at Knebworth House and Bleinheim Palace. The directors of the company were all wealthy railway enthusiasts who would provide the initial funding. However, Pleasurerail was meant to operate on a normal commercial basis, with revenue being generated to keep the company in situ. Work began on the first part of the line in the second half of 1970 with a length of track measuring one thousand feet being laid. This began adjacent to the then Children's Zoo, and ended in the new rhino paddock. In July of that same year the first of the four ex-Bowaters steam locomotives arrived on site, this being an 0-6-2 side tank engine - "Chevallier". This locomotive had been built in 1915 by the Manning Wardle Company, and had worked for the Royal Navy on the Chattenden and Upnor Railway, located near to Chatham Docks. In 1950, "Chevallier" moved to the Bowater Railway after being replaced by diesels. It was on the 26th of August 1970 that this engine had the honour of hauling the first ever train on the WR, this working carrying the grand total of 120 people, including media representatives. As the rhinos based in the paddock had come from Umfolozi, the WR was initially known as the "Whipsnade and Umfolozi Railway". Following the opening, a full daily service was operated until the end of September 1970 and then a reduced winter service was run until Easter 1971.

From the beginning, the railway was a success. As mentioned previously, three other steam locomotives, together with a pair of diesels, came to Whipsnade in 1970 to help run the line. The steamers concerned were "Excelsior", which was an 0-4-2 saddle tank engine built by Kerr Stuart in 1908, "Conqueror", a second 0-6-2 side tank constructed by Bagnell in 1922, and "Superior", a third 0-6-2 tank loco, but this time built by Kerr Stuart in 1920. The coaches used had been made utilising the frames of the wagons bought from Bowaters. They gave passengers a good view of the white rhinos, and, in doing so, fufilled the original objective of those who had brought the WR into being.

In the latter part of 1972, plans were drawn up to convert the railway into a complete circuit. This was the beginning of the line which is in operation today. The construction work was, once again, financed by Pleasurerail and the new line brought into operation in August 1973. As part of this work, the original station was closed, and a new station, Whipsnade Central, was built at the point of the line nearest to the centre of the zoo. The station featured a passing loop, platforms on both lines, together with a signalbox (which had been the booking office at the original station), and a souvenir shop, which doubled up as the booking office. This is very much how the station looks today, except that a separate booking office now exists by the entrance to the platforms. When the original part of the WR was first built, a small engine shed was constructed near to the station and this continued in operation after the full circuit was laid. Both steam and diesel locomotives were (and are) serviced in this area.

The Whipsnade Wildlife Park Railway's main station, with 0-6-2T "Superior"
about to leave, April 2006. (MJE).

Leaving Whipsnade Central on its two mile journey, the present day railway passes the current Children's Zoo and the bird garden on the left of the line. At this point, the site of the original station, and the engine shed, can be seen before the running line swings to the right. On the right hand side of the line can be seen the compound which houses the Asian elephants. A number of these magnificent animals can be seen at any one time, and the train offers as good a vantage point as any. Following this, the new white rhino paddock is entered, and close-ups of these formidable beasts can be seen from the train. Obviously, over many years, the rhinos have become quite used to the trains invading their territory! At this point in the journey, the train is on the opposite side of the circuit from Whipsnade Central. The grasslands are vast, and appear on both sides of the line, the resident animals being made up of a mixture of camels, yak and deer. The line swings right once again, passing the site of the now-closed Umfolozi Halt, which in fact has never been used as a station since its completion in 1974. The route begins to climb at this point and passengers can hear the sound of the engine working hard in order to counter the gradient. After passing through a narrow tunnel, the line swings right for the last time, and passes the "Cafe on the Lake", which is located adjacent to Whipsnade Central station.

For almost forty years the WR has become very successful and a major attraction at the Zoo. Today, it is marketed as the "Jumbo Express", and still operates two of the original quartet of ex-Bowaters steam locomotives. The major change that has occurred since the opening of the complete circuit is that the line is now operated by the Zoo itself, instead of Pleasurerail, the latter having disbanded in 1990. Passenger figures have averaged around 100,000 people per annum during the life of the WR. In conclusion, the WR is a proper working railway, worthy of further study. It appears to be by-passed by many railway enthusiasts and yet it has a charm all of its own. It provides a glimpse of steam locomotives in action in an area that is somewhat barren as far as railway preservation is concerned, apart from the excellent Leighton Buzzard Narrow Gauge Railway, and some miniature railways. Hopefully, its good state of health will provide a basis for future expansion projects.

A "PUBLIC" RAILWAY

THE FANCOTT MINIATURE RAILWAY

Visitors to the Fancott public house, which is based in Fancott, Bedfordshire, may be somewhat surprised to find a miniature railway situated within its grounds. The Fancott Miniature Railway (FMR), (which was known as the Fancott Light Railway (FLR) until 2001), is an impressive attraction in its own right. It is much more than a "toy" railway, being one that is worthy of closer inspection, both by casual passers-by and by railway enthusiasts.

Although there may well have been a miniature railway within the grounds of the Fancott as far back as 1968, the forerunner of the current railway was in situ during the mid 1970s. This system was laid to a 10 & 1/4" gauge, and consisted merely of a straight "out and back" piece of track beginning where the present day station is located, and running to the limit of the section of land owned by the pub. Its sole example of motive power was a petrol engined locomotive named "Fancott 2", the powerplant being an ex-BSA motor bike engine. As there was very little covered accommodation at the site, and, as a result, a lack of security, it is thought that "Fancott 2" was brought in by its owner on each day that the line was operated. At the time, trains only ran on Sundays; however, it must be assumed that passenger numbers on the railway were not as much as had been hoped, because this brave venture was closed in the early 1980s.

For the next decade, it seemed that the failure of the aforementioned railway spelt the end of any thoughts of a miniature line on the site. However, in 1995, the catalyst for the rise of a new railway came in the form of Paul Wallman, who took over as the landlord of the Fancott at this time, and who remains in charge to this day. Using self-generated funds, Mr Wallman employed the services of a local-based model-maker, Richard Bennett, to build a new line, laid to 7 & 1/4" gauge, this being the "standard" width for all railways of this type located in Britain. The second Fancott Light Railway utilised the area of the old line's station to build a new one; this being the beginning of a balloon shaped section of track. At the same time, a signalbox was constructed at the end of the station, and was based on old-fashioned boxes of the steam-age railway, of the type usually found in less busy locations. The new line began operations in 1996, and for the next three years ran successfully without any major problems. However, a crisis arose at the end of the running season in 1999, when Mr Bennett decided to leave the railway.

In order to keep the railway operating, Mr Wallman had to find a replacement for Mr Bennett. The new manager came in the form of Ron Stanbridge, who officially took over the FLR on February 18th 2000. For the first two running seasons, Mr Stanbridge operated the railway that had been built by Mr Bennett. However, during this time, it was clear that major changes would have to be made if the FLR was to continue operations for the foreseeable future. With the help of a fellow enthusiast and model maker, Jim Vass, a plan was drawn up by Mr Stanbridge and agreed with Mr Wallman. During 2001, the name of the FLR was changed to the Fancott Miniature Railway (FMR).

The biggest problem faced at this time was the condition of the track laid in 1995/6. This was laid on welded rail, and it was found that the curves encountered were too tight for one of the locomotives used at this time, "Herbie". This petrol-hydraulic powered locomotive needed to be driven at very low speeds, because of the risk of it becoming derailed. Clearly such a situation could not be allowed to continue. Another problem was that not enough ballast had been used in the laying of the original permanent way. The FMR "masterplan" called for the existing track to be lifted and new rails to be laid. The configuration adopted was that which forms the basis of today's railway. The new railway consisted of an oval shaped piece of track, with a junction leading from

"Herbie", a petrol-engined locomotive, waits patiently for its next load of passengers on the Fancott Minature Railway. Behind the photographer is the triangular junction which leads onto the FMR's main line. In the background, and to the left, is the Fancott public house 26/8/07. (MJE)

the "main line" into the station. The aforementioned junction was laid in the form of a triangle, thus allowing trains to access the rest of the system in both directions. These track laying operations were almost finished by the time the FMR was due to re-open for the 2002 season; this being at Easter time. A team of nine people were employed in the rebuilding of the railway, two of these being Mr Stanbridge himself and his elder son Matthew as full time employees of the railway, the remainder being volunteers. The party met every Tuesday during the re-construction period, the rails, sleepers and points having been sourced from a company in Bristol. For the first week of the 2002 season, a gap measuring three carriage lengths was the only section of line still being re-laid. Trains were operated on the rest of the system with a locomotive at each end - this being known as the "top and tail" method. However, the gap was quickly bridged, and train operations settled down to a more normal pattern.

Under the considerable skill and influence of Mr Stanbridge, the FMR has come on in leaps and bounds since 2002. The circuit of track to be found today is a quarter of a mile in length, and has one claim to fame in that it is reckoned to have the steepest gradient of any miniature railway in Britain, this being 1 in 30, which can be a struggle at times for the locomotives used. The domestic motive power fleet found on the FMR consists of a trio of petrol-engined locomotives. The previously-mentioned "Herbie" is the mainstay of the fleet, having arrived in 2000 from the Southill Miniature Railway, this line being found within the grounds of the "White Horse" public house at Southill, which is located near Biggleswade. This locomotive was originally fitted with a 7 hp engine; however, this has since been replaced by a Honda 5.5 hp powerplant. A single coach arrived at the same time to supplement the carriage fleet, which now stands at a total of three. In the last two years, "Herbie" has clocked up no fewer than 8000 miles, which works out at around 28 miles on each operating day. It is owned by the pub itself, as is "Pippa", a smaller locomotive powered by a 4 hp Japanese engine. The third member of this hard-working trio is 47586 "Northampton", which is a Melgar 6.6 hp engined (and much smaller!) version of Network Rail's long-lived class 47 diesel locomotive fleet. This engine is owned by Mr Stanbridge, and has appeared on gala events at other miniature lines.

The FMR is run as a commercial operation and has a permanent staff of four people, who are rostered in pairs of two, working on alternate weekends during the operating season. There is also a voluntary support group, the "Fancott Miniature Railway Society" (FMRS), the members of which are welcome to come and help on the FMR at any time. The FMRS also provides visiting locomotives. The full operating season begins each year on Mother's Day and extends through to Halloween and the Christmas period, a special train service being run to mark these occasions, the former including "after-dark" services. Throughout the year, special events supplement the regular timetable, the highlight of the year being the annual "Steam Gala", which takes place during the month of June. For this, the FMR plays host to a cross-section of steam engines, with freight workings and double-headed trains being part of the day's events. For modern traction followers, a diesel gala is held each September. The end result of all this considerable activity is that the FMR carries an annual total of some 10,000 passengers, a staggering figure for this type of railway.

The FMR is not content to rest on its laurels, and further plans are being drawn up to build on what is already in situ. The next major project is to be the installation of colour light signals and interlocking points, thus allowing two trains to run on the system at any one time, in complete safety. This scheme will also allow for "bi-directional" running; this means that more than one train can run in either direction round the "main line". Currently, bi-directional running can take place, but only with one train at a time, this being for safety reasons. The FMR has been working hard to publicise itself by becoming a member of an umbrella organisation for miniature railways known as "Britain's Great Little Railways". A family tradition of working on the FMR has already been created. Although Mr Stanbridge's elder son Matthew has left the employment of the railway, his younger brother Ashley has taken his place. Between them, Matthew and Ashley, in their capacity as FMR Website Managers, have created the FMR website, a considerable source of information about the line, this being in addition to their duties on the railway itself. Other schemes will no doubt follow; to borrow a phrase used by the world-famous Romney, Hythe, and Dymchurch Railway based in Kent, to the onlooker it appears that the FMR is hoping to become a "main line in miniature".

To sum up, in a short period of just over a decade, the FMR has grown from a small railway into a major attraction within the locality. As mentioned at the start of this article, it is well worth a closer look. On a hot day, the combination of good food, a pleasant drink, and miniature railway travelling is hard to resist. Check it out!

Website; www.fancottrailway.tk

Website; www.thefancott.co.uk (this is the pub's own website; the FMR has a separate page).

ON THE BORDER

THE WELLINGBOROUGH TO HIGHAM FERRERS BRANCH LINE

A uthor's note; Readers of this chapter will be quite right in thinking that the line which forms the subject of this article is located just on the Northamptonshire side of the Bedfordshire border. However, I felt that the story of this route was an interesting one (with a happy ending), and I would, therefore, like to exercise a little "poetic licence" in including it within the covers of this book.

The remarkable number of railway building schemes that were completed during the course of the nineteenth century, together with the even greater number of plans and proposals that never went further than the drawing board, all came about mainly for one of two reasons. The first reason was due to the fact that the many private railway companies that flourished at the time were always looking out for opportunities to increase revenue by building additional lines. In some cases, such routes led to nothing more than a duplication of the facilities that were already on offer. Whilst many towns and cities found themselves in the enviable position of having a choice of train service, such a situation became unworkable as alternative means of transport became available, especially after the Second World War, when private car ownership reached new levels. Those lines that were found to be uneconomic were cut back on a large scale, mainly beginning in the 1950s, with the process of change being accelerated by the infamous Beeching Report published in the early 1960s.

The second main reason for the rapid expansion of the railway system during the Victorian era was in response to local demands, in particular from tradesmen and businessmen. Such circumstances were the beginnings of the four mile long Wellingborough to Higham Ferrers branch line, which was constructed by the Midland Railway (MR). During the 1880s, those people who originated various businesses in the area (in particular those engaged in the manufacture of footwear, which was the major industry in both Higham Ferrers and Rushden) were somewhat displeased with the location of those railway routes nearest to these areas of production. The lines in question were those running between Peterborough and Blisworth, this being part of the London and North Western Railway (LNWR), and the MR's main line running into London St Pancras, this trunk route taking in the towns of Wellingborough, Irchester, Sharnbrook and Bedford, on its way to the capital. The distance between these railway lines and the shoe-making factories was causing delays in getting the completed footwear, together with other associated products, to the various retail outlets. In response to the pleas of the business owners, an initial plan was drawn up during the 1890s for a secondary route running from Irchester Junction, which was located south of Wellingborough on the MR's main line, to Rushden, Higham Ferrers, and on to Raunds. Here the line would have linked up with a second MR cross-country route, this latter section running between Kettering and Huntingdon. The importance attached to this project was emphasied by the fact that a double track formation was planned for the whole of the new route.

However, a group of people even more powerful than the local businessmen put paid to part of this logical scheme, these being a group of landowners. Not only did they voice their disapproval at the scheme to construct a double track railway, legend has it that one of their number purposely built a row of cottages across the proposed trackbed of the Higham Ferrers to Raunds section. Whether this story is true or not, the properties concerned were placed in an isolated location, and this unorthodox course of action had the desired effect, as this part of the line was never built. It was therefore decided to build the route as an ordinary branch line, only running as far as Higham Ferrers, and featuring a single intermediate station at Rushden. This part of the scheme was authorised

Midland Railway 0-4-4T 58085 heading the 13.00 local passenger train from Wellingborough to Higham Ferrers 5/1/1952. (Courtesy; R.J.Buckley/Initial Photographics).

by an Act of Parliament, the line being opened for goods traffic only in September 1893, whilst a passenger service was inaugurated in May the following year. The service was provided by a "push-pull" type train, an MR tank locomotive being employed with two coaches. For many years thereafter, as with many similar branch lines up and down the length and breadth of Britain, the Higham Ferrers line led an undistinguished life, although it became a more than useful cornerstone in the life of the local economy. However, two external forces led to the gradual dwindling of traffic on the branch, the first being the unstoppable march of private car ownership, together with the growth of lorry and bus transport. The second was the steady decline of local industry, in particular the shoe making factories, much of whose work was lost to overseas locations. The passenger trains were the first to fall victim to these forces, the last such working taking place during June 1959. However, various special workings continued for a few more years until 1964, when this trade was bought to an end. Goods traffic lingered on until 1971, when this too was conceded to road transport.

A former Midland Railway 0-6-0 locomotive, no 43624, is seen at
Wellingborough on 26/9/1957, with a short freight train for Higham Ferrers.
(Courtesy of Mr K.C.H.Fairey).

It seemed for many years as though the Wellingborough-Higham
Ferrers line would become just another forgotten rural railway, lost in
the mists of time. However, although all traces of Higham Ferrers station
quickly vanished beneath a new housing estate, the intermediate station
of Rushden was purchased by Northamptonshire County Council when
the line was finally closed and put to use as a warehouse. Such a shrewd
move ensured that the fine MR buildings survived into the railway
preservation era, and, in turn, attracted the attention of a local voluntary
organisation, the Rushden Historical Transport Society (RHTS) during
the course of the early 1980s. In 1984 the Society concluded a deal with
the County Council to lease these historic buildings on an annual basis.
A threat of demolition in the late 1980s was thankfully avoided, and the
Society purchased the station outright during 1996.

Since that time, the RHTS have established a fine transport museum

The station building at Rushden, part of which acts as a museum for its owners, the Rushden Historical Transport Society (RHTS). A comprehensive restoration programme has been carried out here, and it is a credit to the preservationists concerned 26/8/07. (MJE)

at the station, the former parcels office, ticket office, and waiting room having all been converted for this purpose. One room concentrates on road transport, with items such as road signs, maps and associated street furniture combining to make up a display full of interest. The other two rooms are given over to railway related artefacts, with such things as railway uniforms, "totem" station signs, and model locomotives being found, together with a comprehensive collection of photographs providing a pictorial history of the branch and serving as inspiration for the future. Further along the platform can be found the Victorian Bar, a refuge for many a thirsty traveller, and the source of a further collection of historical railway photographs. The single platform is host to a running line one quarter of a mile long. It is hoped that a light railway order will be granted at a date not too distant to enable passenger services to begin once again. A signal box can be found further along this section of track, along with various items of rolling stock. Although the array of sidings that made up the former goods yard have vanished beneath a new road, the goods shed is still in situ, and currently serves as a warehouse. It is seen as a possible future acquisition for the Society. The museum is open every Sunday from March to October between 10.30am and 16.00 for viewing purposes.

The former goods shed at Rushden, currently in use as a private stores department. This is located across the road in the foreground from the main station building at Rushden station 26/8/07. (MJE)

What of the future? Although the Society's ultimate aim is to re-open the whole of the branch to Wellingborough, a more realistic aim is to head in the opposite direction towards Higham Ferrers, which is only three quarters of a mile away. As mentioned before, the site of the original station is now part of a housing estate; however, the RHTS would like to get as close as they can to the original site and construct a new station there. One major problem standing in the way of the Wellingborough extension is the absence of a bridge spanning the road running at right angles to the station, this having been demolished in the years since closure. Some parts of the former trackbed have been converted to public footpaths, whilst others have been incorporated into private property or become part of roads. Although it would appear to many observers that such a scheme would be a long one, with the right amount of voluntary and financial support there is no reason why it should not happen, given enough time. It should be remembered that even the well known preserved railways of the present day, such as the Severn Valley Railway, were in exactly the same situation when their respective restoration projects began.

Riddles designed locomotive, 2-6-2 tank locomotive 84006, which is depicted at Rushden station on 28/5/1959 with the branch line train.
(Courtesy of Mr K.C.H.Fairey).

In summing up, it is refreshing to report that rather than the story of the Wellingborough-Higham Ferrers branch being one of a railway line that enjoyed a brief heyday, but which then faded away, it is a story that promises to get better and better, with the route hopefully coming back to life, reminding future generations of a significant part of the local area's industrial history.

THE RUSHDEN HISTORICAL TRANSPORT SOCIETY

Contact Address: Rushden Transport Museum, Station Approach, Rushden, Northants. NN10 0AW.

Telephone: 01933-350415 & 01933-411070.

Website: www.rhts.co.uk

FOR THE ENTHUSIAST

LCGB Bedford Branch members and friends enjoying the sunshine outside Euston station whilst awaiting a visit to the nearby London Underground control centre circa 1980s. Left to right; Kevin Darnell (visitor), David Smith (Branch Treasurer), The Jones Twins plus a friend, Chris Jones (Branch Chairman), Martin Parker (member), the late Jack Butcher (Branch Fixtures Officer) and the late John Dolamore (Branch Librarian).
(Courtesy of Mr Bryan Cross).

THE BEDFORD BRANCH OF
THE LOCOMOTIVE CLUB OF
GREAT BRITAIN

A SHORT HISTORY

The current railway scene within the county of Bedfordshire is a very healthy one indeed. At the time of writing, two main lines pass within its borders, these being the East Coast Main Line beginning at London Kings Cross, and the Midland route, which commences at the upgraded St Pancras station. This is not to be confused with the former London Midland route which starts from Euston. Although the county saw the closure of a number of branch lines during the dark days of the 1950s and 1960s, the middle section of the London and North Western Railway's (LNWR) cross-country line between Oxford and Cambridge, that being the route from Bletchley to Bedford, remains open. Preservation is also in evidence, with the splendid Leighton Buzzard Narrow Gauge Railway being the heritage "jewel in the crown" within the county, along with the Whipsnade Wild Animal Park Railway, whilst the Buckinghamshire Railway Centre, together with the Chinnor and Princes Risborough Railway, can be found within neighbouring counties. Local clubs are also in evidence, one of the most active of which is the Bedford Branch of the Locomotive Club of Great Britain (LCGB).

The origins of the Branch go back to 1958. At that time, the local railway scene was very much as it had always been, with steam in command, and a healthy series of lines, both trunk and secondary, still running, Bedford itself being at the centre of much of this activity. However, significant changes commenced during this year, when diesel multiple units began to appear on some routes. It was this change that

Higham Ferrers station is the location for this view of an LCGB Bedford Branch brake van special train, hauled by Riddles designed 2-6-0 locomotive 78028, and taken on 3/7/1965. (Courtesy of Mr K.C.H.Fairey).

inspired a group of local railway enthusiasts to form a Bedford Branch of the LCGB. The LCGB itself had been founded in 1949 as an organisation initially catering for both number takers and model makers. However, by the end of the 1950s, it had re-invented itself as a group catering for the more serious study of railways. It was fortunate that the fledgling Branch was able to call upon the services of the LCGB's "Member No One", Mr Jack Turner, the man who was the catalyst for the founding of the Club at Aylesbury some nine years earlier. He became the first Branch Chairman and was instrumental in steering the group through its early years.

The Branch settled into a pattern of organising "seasons" of indoor lectures on railway related subjects, a pattern which continues to this day. In the early years, subjects covered were mainly of a steam-related nature, although other topics could be found within a year's programme. From 1958 to 1963, meetings were held at the Grosvenor Club (later to be known as the Grosvenor Centre), a working man's club situated within Bedford. After a break between 1963 and 1965, meetings recommenced at this location until the early 1980s.

Outdoor activities became a feature of the Branch's curriculum as the 1950s gave way to the 1960s. The decline of steam on the national railway network was gathering pace, and "shed-bashing" visits were organised by the Branch on a periodic basis between 1964 and 1968. Participants concentrated on a particular geographical area and used either private cars or hired minibuses to access the sheds in question. An example of one of these visits was a single day's trip on 20/12/1964, this being in a south-westerly direction, and taking in the sheds at Weymouth, Bristol Barrow Road, Bath Green Park, Radstock, Westbury, Yeovil, and Templecombe. The "score" for this busy day was 127 steam and 17 diesel locomotives seen. Over the next few years, even more complex plans were organised and carried out, the major trips at this time taking in such areas as Scotland, the North East, and to the last stronghold of British steam, this being in the North West of England. The Branch also began to organise its own rail tours, these taking in local routes, in some cases, before these succumbed to the march of modernisation. An early example of this activity took place on 3/7/1965, when a train made up of brake vans was used to tour over various branch lines in the county of Northamptonshire. Such lines included the Wellingborough to Higham Ferrers line (related in more detail elsewhere with this book), and the Kettering to Loddington route. This latter visit was somewhat of a struggle due to the severe gradient that was encountered soon after leaving Kettering. After two fruitless attempts to ascend this bank, it was decided that the ten brake vans which made up the train would have to be reduced to four to order to get over the 1 in 44 incline. Returning to Kettering, the six surplus vehicles were uncoupled from the train, and it was "third time lucky" as the train's engine, a Riddles designed 2-6-0 tender locomotive, no 78028, plus the remaining four vans, made it over the gradient and along the four mile line to the out-of-use loading dock at Loddington.

An enduring feature of the history of the Bedford Branch is the annual quiz between LCGB Bedford and the Northampton Branch of the Railway Correspondence and Travel Society (RCTS). In more recent years, the competition has been expanded by the inclusion of two more teams, in the form of LCGB St Albans and RCTS Milton Keynes. For many years the quizzes have been held twice per year, Bedford being the venue in the spring, whilst the "return" is played at Northampton during the autumn. The quizzes have been given an extra flavour by the fact that a trophy is played for, this being known as the "Ashes". This is not the legendary "Ashes" of cricketing fame, but the remains of the former signalbox at Ravenstone Junction, which was situated near to Northampton. A suitable trophy was built to house these ashes, and it has remained in use as the main prize for almost forty years. Apart from the element of competition, and the chance for some brainwork, the quiz acts as a good social event, and helps to maintain contact between the different railway societies.

The programme of indoor meetings continued during the 1970s, still taking place at the Grosvenor Centre. By the time of the 1977 Annual General Meeting (AGM), the average meeting attendance was now around the forty mark, with a figure of no fewer than 94 people turning up for a lecture on "Steam Cinema" films during 1979. However, at this time, concern was being expressed at the long term financial stability of the Branch, one of the reasons for this being the cost of travelling to Bedford for some members. This reduced numbers at the meetings, and, after an Extraordinary General Meeting (EGM) in late 1981, it was decided to move the meetings from the Grosvenor Centre to a less expensive venue, the Southend Working Men's Club (SWMC). The 1980s were times of struggle for the Branch. However, a bright note was struck by the marking of the 25th Anniversary of the foundation of the Branch in July 1983 with the running of a private train on the Peterborough based Nene Valley Railway, an event which was attended by more than one hundred people. This event proved that there was still a need for an LCGB Branch in Bedford, and, over the next few years, meetings continued to be held at the SWMC. However, this venue was closed in December 1991, and the Branch was forced to find alternative accommodation. The Branch was to be fortunate in this respect, as one of its members, Alan Ledwick, had connections with the St Johns Church in

Bedford, and suggested that the Branch might like to move its meetings there. This idea was taken up, the first gathering at the new venue being in January 1992. In previous years, meetings had always been held on a Monday night; prior commitments at the new venue meant that Tuesday became the new meeting night. The Branch has continued to meet here to the present day.

Under the enthusiastic and energetic direction of its current chairman/secretary Bryan Cross, today's Bedford Branch continues to enjoy healthy attendances at its monthly lectures. Meetings are held each month, except for August, when the Branch committee take a well-earned break. The Branch AGM is held each September, when a guest speaker is invited to supplement the formal business, whilst the "Ashes" quiz and a "Christmas Special" add variety to the more conventional talks on offer. Outdoor activities include visits to local preserved railways, whilst fund raising stands are arranged at model railway exhibitions within Bedford's catchment area. These latter activities, as well as raising much needed pennies, help to keep the Branch in the public eye, attracting new members whilst retaining a miscellany of older ones. A Branch photographic competition is organised, whilst members can enjoy discounts on new railway books, videos and DVDs from two leading makers of these items.

In conclusion, the future of the Bedford Branch of the LCGB looks very bright. Although over the years, it has had some ups and downs, rather like the railways of the local area, it has survived and has become stronger as a result. It keeps the LCGB flag flying within the county and encourages railway interest, furthering serious study of this great subject. Long may it continue to do so!

Meetings held at; The St Johns Church Hall, St Johns Street, Bedford.

When ?; First Tuesday of every month (except August), beginning at 19.30 hours.

Admission; 50p for LCGB members, £1.00 for non-members.

Contact Phone; 01525-750149 or 01933-273373.

Website; http://www.lcgb.net (The Branch has its own page).

THE RAILWAY AGE IN BEDFORDSHIRE

F G Cockman

Since it was first published in 1974 Fred Cockman's book has remained the classic history of the railway age in Bedfordshire in one volume. His book traces the early development of the railway network in the County from 1837 and there are separate chapters on the schemes that failed, contractors and navvies, railway accidents and railway crime.

Fred Cockman, who has lived in Bedford since 1938, is a well-known railway historian and has many books and articles to his name. This welcome second edition, which includes many fresh illustrations, will appeal to anyone interested in Bedfordshire railways at a time when privatisation means that the whole network has reached another turning point in its history.

Book
Castle
PUBLISHING

THE LIFE AND TIMES OF THE GREAT EASTERN RAILWAY

Harry Paar   Adrian Gray

This book is a unique collection of stories about the personalities involved with the Great Eastern Railway; the directors, management, staff and passengers of this East Anglian railway network. From the period of its inception in 1839, through to its absorption into the LNER in 1923, it tells of the enthusiasm, the incompetence, the board room struggles and chicanery, tragic accidents and other incidents in its history.

Harry Paar and Adrian Gray capture the life and times of those early years by their diligent research of the contemporary press; the stories brought to life by the work of press artists and photographers of the period. With pictures and old Ordnance Survey maps they show how the railway transformed so many towns and villages of East Anglia in the late nineteenth century.

'TIS THE FAR FAMOUS VALE
National Influences on the Vale of Aylesbury

Ken and Margaret Morley

Much local history is determined (or at least influenced) by national and international events, and the Vale is no exception. This is a really well-informed and well-written account of the ways in which history and the waves of change have swept through the Vale. Over the last 1600 years its tranquillity has repeatedly been shattered by outside infl uences such as: war and disease; the ambitions of royalty; the search for wealth in this life, and a place beside the Almighty in the next; the inspiration of inventors in agriculture and industry; and the import and export of people and goods. Fortunately, there is an increasing realisation that local history cannot be fully appreciated unless national factors are taken into account, and this factor is at the heart of the present volume.

As with their earlier books, the Morleys' story has been enhanced by numerous illustrations:150 black and white pictures, 40 colour photographs, 16 maps and diagrams, 32 tables, numerous contemporary quotations and 13 longer Recollections. Wherever possible these are the views of ordinary people in their own words. 37 worthwhile visits are also suggested, so that readers can add reality to the word pictures.

This is essentially a book for adults, but it will also be particularly relevant to students facing examinations which (we are assured) will increasingly be focussed on English history.

The following twenty-two towns, villages and sites are amongst the forty-nine used to illustrate and authenticate the information in the text.

Aylesbury, Brill, Buckingham, Cuddington, Haddenham, Hulcott, Leighton & Linslade, Long Crendon, Notley Abbey, Pitstone, Quarrendon, Princes Risborough, Soulbury, Stewkley, Thame, Waddesdon, Wendover, Whitchurch, Wing, Wingrave, Winslow.

All the above, and the twenty-seven not in the list, are included in the book's very full index.

BLETCHLEY PARK'S SECRET SISTERS
Psychological Warfare in World War 11

John A. Taylor

Bletchley Park will be forever associated with the secret intelligence activities of World War Two. Yet in addition to the incredible achievements of the code breakers, only a few miles away several other secret organisations were also achieving clandestine success, with operations that were conducted from centres hidden in the local countryside. This region had been chosen by the Government because it was remote from the London Blitz yet still maintained good road and rail communications with the Capital - but what did these secret organisations do?

In a highly subversive campaign, propaganda playcd an early and effective role, selecting recruits from amongst the refugees fleeing Nazi oppression. Gathered in large, local houses, there they would write and rehearse propaganda scripts for radio broadcasts to enemy territory. At a secret studio, these broadcasts were then recorded onto discs and taken by the Secret Service to radio transmitting stations, hidden in the local countryside.

Under the control of the Communications Section of the Secret Intelligence Service, another radio station transmitted decoded information from Bletchley Park to Allied military commanders overseas. Further radio stations maintained contact with secret agents, sent on missions deep inside Occupied Europe. In hidden workshops, advanced radio equipment for their use was designed and manufactured and in various country houses specialised training schools were set up.

Later in the war, not far from Woburn Abbey an ultra modern recording and broadcast studio was then built which, when linked to the most powerful radio transmitter in Europe, began use in sophisticated operations that would completely deceive and confuse the Germans.

This book now tells the little known story of all these other secret activities, the fascinating story of Bletchley Park's 'Secret Sisters'.

BERNARD WEST'S BEDFORDSHIRE

Edited by Gordon Vowles

This book is made up of a selection of Bernard West's Sketch-book of drawings and comment which appeared in the Bedfordshire Magazine over a fifty year period from 1947. The sketches are of village and townscapes or of individual buildings or features spread throughout the whole of the County of Bedfordshire. Each sketch is accompanied by a lively commentary which displays Bernard West's wide-ranging knowledge of the County, its history and its buildings, and his keen interest, as a professional architect, in good design and the preservation of both the natural and the man-made environments. The volume is a tribute to a gifted artist and an ardent campaigner.

It is a book which should have a wide appeal, but especially to those who have an interest in Bedfordshire's past and its continued preservation.

JOURNEYS INTO BEDFORDSHIRE
JOURNEYS INTO BUCKINGHAMSHIRE
JOURNEYS INTO HERTFORDSHIRE

Anthony Mackay

These three books of ink drawings reveal an intriguing historic heritage and capture the spirit of England's rural heartland, ranging widely over cottages and stately homes, over bridges, churches and mills, over sandy woods, chalk downs and watery river valleys.

Every corner of Bedfordshire, Buckinghamshire and Hertfordshire has been explored in the search for material, and, although the choice of subjects is essentially a personal one, the resulting collection represents a unique record of the environment today.

The notes and maps, which accompany the drawings, lend depth to the books, and will assist others on their own journeys around the counties.

Anthony Mackay's pen-and-ink drawings are of outstanding quality. An architectural graduate, he is equally at home depicting landscapes and buildings. The medium he uses is better able to show both depth and detail than any photograph.

265

FORGOTTEN FAMILIES
of Hertfordshire and Bedfordshire

Evelyn Wright

This book tells the story of families once famous but whose fame is now mainly forgotten. They all lived in Hertfordshire and Bedfordshire in the 16th and 17th centuries, and include the Bechers of Renhold (of Becher's Brook fame), the Mordaunts of Turvey Abbey, Lady Cathcart of Tewin, the Bull family of Hertford, the Nodes family of Stevenage, the Docuras of Lilley and the Wicked Lady of Markyate Cell. All the families were related to each other, forming an intricate network over two counties: Hertfordshire and Bedfordshire. The author is one of their 20th century descendants. The book includes pedigrees showing the relationship between various families, and illustrations of many of the manor houses and mansions in which they lived.

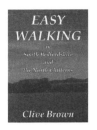

EASY WALKING
in South Bedfordshire and the North Chilterns

Clive Brown

The Northern Chilterns and the southern part of Bedfordshire are a well kept secret. While other areas and regions of this country have a deserved reputation for being excellent walking country, this part of the world has hidden away, guarding its beauty and its diversity. Thick wooded slopes, rolling chalk downland, steep hillsides with terrific views at the top. Tranquil towpaths alongside canals with the occasional narrowboat chugging past. Peaceful undulating farmland and sleepy picturesque villages. The major drawback with this book is that more of the public will come and enjoy it.

The book presents a comprehensive guide to the best walks in this locality; the routes use paths, bridleways, rights of way, National Trails and canal towpaths. Some background information and nature notes are included after the walk directions. All the walks are circular; some are in areas already popular with walkers, others are in areas less popular and perhaps less accessible.

The area covered in this book is dominated by the chalk ridge escarpment of the Chiltern Hills. Not particularly high in comparison to other ranges of hills in this country, they nevertheless tower over the flatter land to the north and the lower south eastern end of the Greensand Ridge around Woburn.

Book Castle
PUBLISHING

267

  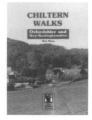

CHILTERN WALKS
Hertfordshire, Bedfordshire and North Buckinghamshire

CHILTERN WALKS
Buckinghamshire

CHILTERN WALKS
Oxfordshire and West Buckinghamshire

Nick Moon

A series of three books to providing a comprehensive coverage of walks throughout the whole of the Chiltern area (as defined by the Chiltern Society). The walks included vary in length from 3.0 to 10.9 miles, but are mainly in the 5-7 mile range popular for half-day walks, although suggestions of possible combinations of walks are given for those preferring a full day's walk.

Each walk gives details of nearby places of interest and is accompanied by a specially drawn map of the route which also indicates local pubs and a skeleton road network.

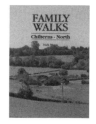 

FAMILY WALKS
Chilterns – North

FAMILY WALKS
Chilterns - South

Nick Moon

A series of two books providing a comprehensive coverage of walks throughout the whole of the Chiltern area. The walks included vary in length from 1.7 to 5.5 miles, but are mainly in the 3 to 5 mile range, which is ideal for families with children, less experienced walkers or short winter afternoons.

Each walk text gives details of nearby places of interest and is accompanied by a specially drawn map of the route, which also indicates local pubs and a skeleton road network.

The author, Nick Moon, has lived in or regularly visited the Chilterns all his life and has for 25 years, been an active member of the Chiltern Society's Rights of Way Group, which seeks to protect and improve the area's footpath and bridleway network.

PUB WALKS FROM COUNTRY STATIONS
Volume 1 - Beds and Herts

PUB WALKS FROM COUNTRY STATIONS
Volume 2 - Bucks and Oxon

Clive Higgs

Two titles both containing fourteen circular country rambles, each starting and finishing at a railway station and incorporating a pub-stop at a mid-way point.

Volume 1 has 5 walks in Bedfordshire starting from Sandy, Biggleswade, Harlington, Flitwick and Linslade. Together with 9 walks in Hertfordshire starting from Watford, Kings Langley, Boxmoor, Berkhamsted, Tring, Stanstead St. Margaret's, Watton-at-Stone, Bricket Wood and Harpdenden.

Volume 2 has 9 walks in Buckingham starting from Gerrards Cross, Beaconsfield, Saunderton, Princes Risborough, Amersham, Chesham, Great Missenden, Stoke Manderville and Wendover. Together with 5 walks in Oxfordshire starting from Goring-on-Thames, Cholsey, Lower Shiplake, Islip and Hanborough Station.

The shortest walk is a distance of 4 miles and the longest 7 and a half miles.

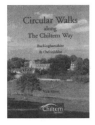

CIRCULAR WALKS ALONG THE CHILTERN WAY

Volume One Buckinghamshire and Oxfordshire

Volume Two Hertfordshire and Bedfordshire

Nick Moon

A two volume series with special maps provided for each walk.

The walks range from 4.3 to 8.5 miles which makes for a comfortable half day or a leisurely full day walk. In addition, details of several possible combinations of walks of up to 22 miles are provided for those who would like a longer, more challenging walk.

Each walk gives details of nearby places of interest and is accompanied by a specially drawn map of the rout which also indicates local pubs and a skeleton road network.

Book Castle
PUBLISHING

THE CHILTERNS
Area of Outstanding Natural Beauty

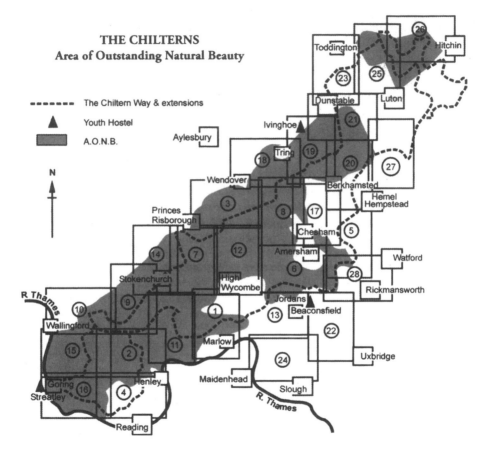

This expanding series of currently 28 maps at a scale of 2½ inches to the mile depicts footpaths, bridleways and other routes available to walkers, riders and cyclists across the Chilterns, as well as pubs, railway stations, car parking facilities and other features of interest. Several suggested walks also appear on the back of each map. New titles appear regularly and will extend coverage of the area.

COMPLETE LIST OF CHILTERN SOCIETY FOOTPATH MAPS

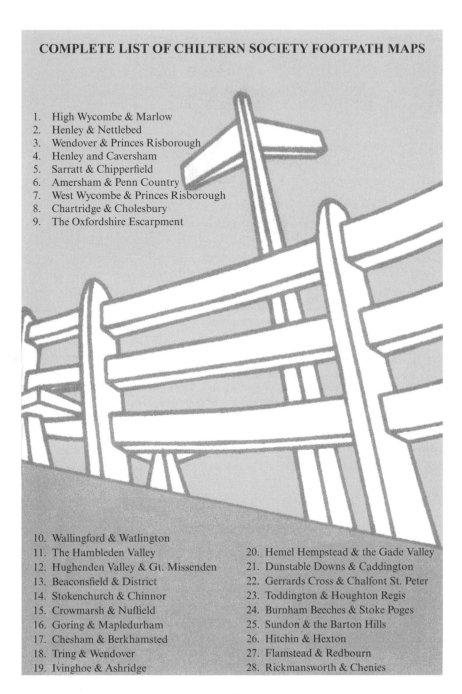

1. High Wycombe & Marlow
2. Henley & Nettlebed
3. Wendover & Princes Risborough
4. Henley and Caversham
5. Sarratt & Chipperfield
6. Amersham & Penn Country
7. West Wycombe & Princes Risborough
8. Chartridge & Cholesbury
9. The Oxfordshire Escarpment

10. Wallingford & Watlington
11. The Hambleden Valley
12. Hughenden Valley & Gt. Missenden
13. Beaconsfield & District
14. Stokenchurch & Chinnor
15. Crowmarsh & Nuffield
16. Goring & Mapledurham
17. Chesham & Berkhamsted
18. Tring & Wendover
19. Ivinghoe & Ashridge

20. Hemel Hempstead & the Gade Valley
21. Dunstable Downs & Caddington
22. Gerrards Cross & Chalfont St. Peter
23. Toddington & Houghton Regis
24. Burnham Beeches & Stoke Poges
25. Sundon & the Barton Hills
26. Hitchin & Hexton
27. Flamstead & Redbourn
28. Rickmansworth & Chenies

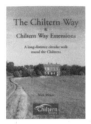

THE CHILTERN WAY & CHILTERN WAY EXTENSIONS
A long-distance circular walk round the Chilterns

Nick Moon

This is an official guide to the now extended circular long distance path through Bedfordshire, Buckinghamshire, Hertfordshire and Oxfordshire.

The Chiltern Way was established by the Chiltern Society to mark the Millennium by providing walkers in the twenty first century with a new way of exploring diverse, beautiful countryside which all four Chiltern counties have to offer. Based on the idea of the late Jimmy Parson's Chiltern Hundred, but expanded to cover the whole Chilterns, the route has been designed by the author and has been signposted, waymarked and improved by the Society's Rights of Way Group.

The northern extension includes walks through the Barton and Pegsdon Hills with superb views over the coombes of Watergutter and Cow holes. The southern extension in Oxfordshire leaves the original route near Maidensgrove and goes on to Goring and then on to Woodcote and Hailey to rejoin the Chiltern Way near Ewelme.

EXPLORING HISTORY ALL AROUND

Vivienne Evans

A handbook of local history, arranged as a series of routes to cover Bedfordshire and adjoining parts of Hertfordshire and Buckinghamshire. It is organised as two books in one. There are seven thematic sections full of fascinating historical detail and anecdotes for armchair reading. Also it is a perfect source of family days out as the book is organised as circular motoring/cycling explorations, highlighting attractions and landmarks. Also included is a background history to all the major towns in the area, plus dozens of villages, which will enhance your appreciation and understanding of the history that is all around you!

275

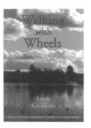

WALKING WITH WHEELS
in Bedfordshire and Milton Keynes

Lynda Kynnersley

Access. The walks have all been chosen for their ease of access with as much information as possible about the physical features of the route, to enable people with limited mobility to decide for themselves whether a particular walk is within their ability. Some walks are on trails that have been specially adapted to make them more accessible but others are on country paths, which have reasonably flat, smooth and hard surfaces.

Distance. The walks vary in length from a mile and a half up to seven miles, with the possibility of extending them to up to fourteen miles. The majority of the walks are designed to be circular with different outward and return routes, but in a few cases there are no suitable return routes and the directions will say to retrace your steps to the start point. A few walks are described as linear and on these routes, you can either do the whole walk, arranging transport at each end, or start the walk at any suitable point, go as far as you choose and retrace your route..

Details of how to get to the start point, where to park and where to find refreshments are all included, as well as general information of interest about the area and what wildlife you may see - everything in fact for a good trip out.

276